IN
HIS
IMAGE

by Sam Polson

God Bless You!

Sam Polson

II Co - 4:5

IN HIS IMAGE

by Sam Polson

Introduction by Al Cage

Afterword by Joe Kappel

Edited by Lisa Soland

Publishing
Angel
Climbing

IN HIS IMAGE

Written by Sam Polson

Introduction by Al Cage

Afterword by Joe Kappel

Edited by Lisa Soland

Text copyright © 2017 Sam Polson

Published in 2017 by:
Climbing Angel Publishing
P.O. Box 32381
Knoxville, Tennessee 37930
http://www.ClimbingAngel.com

First Edition September 2017
Printed in the United States of America
Cover and Logo design by Zachary Hodges
Interior design by Climbing Angel Publishing

ISBN: 978-0-9965721-9-4
Library of Congress Control Number: 2017948121

This book is dedicated to my brother,
Lloyd Polson (1949-2017)
who, in spite of his significant mental
and physical disabilities, was the finest example
of a life lived *In His Image*
that I have ever known.

CONTENTS

PREFACE

W hen I was a boy, on occasion my father would take me to Illinois to visit his side of the family. Most of them originated from the hills of Kentucky but had lived and farmed in Illinois during my dad's young adulthood, primarily during the depression.

After my father became a Christian, he wanted to go back to his childhood community and find as many friends as he could, and tell them what the Lord had done for him. Those are great memories of my life being with my dad when he would intentionally talk with someone about Christ. My father had a joyful trust in the Lord. Even in hardships, he saw life as a gift, and his spirit was contagious.

I remember on one of those occasions we had traveled to Illinois, and my father wanted to see one of the men he had worked with in the corn fields during the depression. He located this man and had a time of sharing with him about the Lord. When he introduced me to this elderly man whose eye sight was failing, the man asked me to come closer. I stood before him and he put his hands on my shoulders and stared intently into my face. He then looked at my dad and I'll never forget his remark. He said, "Luther, as long as that boy lives you will never die."

As a boy, I didn't understand that at first but then I started thinking about it and began to understand that I looked like my father. Quite frankly, it was a bit discouraging because I never thought of my dad as a handsome man. But I want to tell you something, as I grew, my dad grew too. Have you had that experience? I'm always amazed at how much my father learned while I was away at college. As I grew, my dad grew. He grew in my eyes. And I came to the realization that I was glad that I looked like him. But I also had a goal to *be* like him. I wanted to bear his image on the inside as well.

In this book *In His Image*, I would like to encourage us to open our hearts and our minds to the incredible calling and privilege that every child of God has on their life. Each and every one of us has the calling and privilege to bear our Father's image. Our *heavenly* Father.

Maybe as you think of your *Earthly* father, difficult memories come to mind. Or maybe you are blessed as I am to have many fond memories. Regardless of whatever the father image might be in your *physical* existence, we all absolutely have the same Father in our *spiritual* existence. And the great calling in our life, the great privilege, the great purpose in our life, is to bear his image.

I believe this to be the reason the Lord has put this topic so strongly on my heart. Our personal identity, who we are, our perspective of others, our outlook on life, our world view, our purpose, "Why am I here?" "Why was I born?" "Why am I on this planet?" and all the priorities that flow out of that, are anchored in this idea that we are bearing the image of God. There is nothing bigger than this. Nothing. There is nothing more important to a Christian than knowing and understanding God's purpose in their life as his image bearer.

In His Image contains seven chapters followed by thought-provoking guidelines to inspire self-study or community sharing. We call it the R.E.A.P. system and it means simply this: "R" is for the *reading* of suggested Scripture. "E" is for the *examining* of that Scripture. "A" prompts discussion or study on how we might *apply* those principals to our lives, and "P" represents *prayer*, which is an effective way to solidify learning and ask for God's blessing on all that has been explored.

The purpose of this book, *In His Image*, is to deepen your understanding of the purpose for which you were created—to reflect the image of God. Relentlessly pursuing our Creator's purpose is the key to experiencing life as it was meant to be.

Sam Polson
Knoxville, Tennessee
August, 2017

INTRODUCTION

We are all God's image bearers. This fact has nothing to do with one's religion, nationality, economic status, race, or even political party preference. It's no surprise, though, that sin gets in our way of accepting this fundamental truth. But the fact remains the same—everyone is created in God's image. All people. Each and every one of us.

Jesus Christ, the second Adam, was God's *perfect* image bearer. Through his perfectly lived life, Jesus gives to his followers the opportunity to renew what was impacted by Adam's sin. Through the process of sanctification, God restores our status as his image bearers on Earth. We become equipped to see every human being with new eyes—eyes that have been opened to the reality of how precious every human being is to God.

Unfortunately, those who find themselves in positions

of power and privilege are prone to adopt the mantle that God has bestowed a special dispensation of his image upon them. *In His Image* will challenge this way of thinking for any who claim Jesus Christ as their Lord and Savior.

In Acts 10:1-28, we have a story about a dream that was given by God to a Gentile and a Jew. The *Gentile*, Cornelius, is a God-fearer who is devoted to serving God. God honors Cornelius with a dream which initially causes Cornelius great fear. But after recovering from that fear, Cornelius acts and responds in obedience to God.

Meanwhile, Peter, a *Jew*, an Apostle and pillar of the church, is confronted in a dream about some beliefs that are not consistent with God's purpose. He awakens with the understanding that there are certain things that must change. God then brings these two people together so that they may participate as co-equals in God's purpose. In Acts 10:25-28, they meet:

> When Peter entered, Cornelius met him and fell
> down at his feet and worshiped him. But Peter
> lifted him up, saying, "Stand up; I too am a
> man." And as he talked with him, he went in
> and found many persons gathered. And he said
> to them, "You yourselves know how unlawful it
> is for a Jew to associate with or to visit anyone
> of another nation, but God has shown me that I
> should not call any person common or unclean."

Peter is shown by God to respect God's image in someone who is significantly different from him—a Gentile! When we respect God's image in all people, we have the privilege to live God's plan, which is so much grander than our own.

Adam and Eve had no idea of the significant implications their one act of disobedience would have on all of God's creation. In one selfish move, God's plan of every individual respecting each other was shattered. Unfortunately, in a shattered world, it's *people* who get to determine what gives someone value. Maybe someone's value is determined by how much money they make, or on which side of the tracks they live, or who they voted for, or if they graduated from Princeton or from the school of hard knocks. Sometimes people, in a fallen world, know just what it takes to disrespect the image of God in anyone who is different from them.

As believers, we must remember that we are image bearers because we have been bought with a price. We're no longer our own. We are image bearers because we know that God didn't choose us because we were better than anybody else. We recognize that "while we were still sinners, Christ died for us" (Romans 5:8).

In the first chapter of *In His Image*, Sam Polson discusses God's image recognized, and that every person, from conception to final breath, is made in the image of God. The second chapter covers how that image has been ruined by sin. In chapters three and four, Sam discusses God's plan for redeeming his image. God made a promise that he would send another image bearer, Jesus, and by his atoning sacrifice he would redeem us from the curse. Chapters 5, 6, and 7, reveal how God's plan of a complete renewal is actualized—through Jesus, for us, in us, and with our cooperation.

In Acts 10, God shows Peter and Cornelius that they are co-equals in *his* plan. Through Christ, we are able to begin envisioning God's plan for us today. It's in God's plan that representatives from all people of the Earth come to embrace the gospel of Jesus Christ. God is extending that invitation to everyone. All people. Each and every one of us.

Al Cage
Pastor of Community Care
West Park Baptist Church
Knoxville, Tennessee

PART 1: IN HIS IMAGE

1

REFLECTING THE FAIREST OF ALL

L et's begin by laying the foundation of what it means to be made in the image of God. To do so, we will begin in the beginning—Genesis Chapter one. Here, God gives the account of the creation of mankind and mankind's purpose as his image bearers.

> Then God said, "Let us make man in our image, after our likeness. And let them have dominion over the fish of the sea and over the birds of the heavens and over the livestock and over all the earth and over every creeping thing that creeps on the earth."

So God created man in his own image,
in the image of God he created him;
male and female he created them.

And God blessed them. And God said to
them, "Be fruitful and multiply and fill the earth
and subdue it, and have dominion over the fish
of the sea and over the birds of the heavens and
over every living thing that moves on the earth."
And God said, "Behold, I have given you every
plant yielding seed that is on the face of all the
earth, and every tree with seed in its fruit. You
shall have them for food. And to every beast of
the earth and to every bird of the heavens and to
everything that creeps on the earth, everything
that has the breath of life, I have given every
green plant for food." And it was so. And God
saw everything that he had made, and behold, it
was very good. And there was evening and there
was morning, the sixth day. (Genesis 1:26-31)

Imagine having as your purpose, to bear the image of
God. What does it mean to be God's image bearer? Notice
this amazing verse. "Then God said, 'Let us make man in
our image, after our likeness'" (Genesis 1:26). God's intent
for mankind is wrapped up in those words: "image" and
"likeness."

IMAGE AND LIKENESS

Man being created in the image of God is not something that can be fully understood because, after all, we're talking about God. Volumes of theology and philosophy have been written on this subject. So, the idea of being made in his image, to some extent, is indefinable.

Perhaps the best way to approach this is to think about the way the words were first used by God when he said that he made mankind in his image and likeness. What can we understand from that? The word "image" and the word "likeness" are used interchangeably in the Old Testament. Their meaning is very close. Slightly different ideas are behind them, but the words can be used interchangeably.

The word "image" is the Hebrew word *Tselem*. In the Old Testament Tselem is almost always used in a negative connotation where God repeatedly warns his people not to make anything in his image. They were not to make anything that represented God or some other false god that was intended to be worshiped or revered.

The word "likeness" is the Hebrew word *Demuth*, and it has the idea of being similar to the original, not identical, but similar. From the meaning of these two words there are two basic concepts that emerge with regard to what it means that God created mankind in his image and according to his likeness.

HUMAN BEINGS ARE LIKE GOD

Apart from sin, human beings are like God. In the chapters to come, we'll discuss how sin has distorted the image of God in man, but man does still retain the image of God. So, human beings are like God. However, God is not physical so this likeness does not refer to our physical bodies. God is Spirit. Human beings are like God in spirit. But because we have physical bodies, we help to make God's invisible attributes, visible.

Human beings were created, in part, to make God's invisible attributes, visible.

Those attributes of God which can be shared are displayed in human beings.

HUMAN BEINGS REPRESENT GOD

We also learn that we are not only like God, but human beings also represent God. "Let us make man in our image, after our likeness" (Genesis 1:26). We represent God in relation to the rest of what God has created. Mankind is distinct from the rest of creation and we've been given rule over all that God has made. God said, "… have dominion over the fish of the sea and over the birds of the heavens and over every living thing that moves on the earth" (Genesis 1:28). In 1 Corinthians 6, we are reminded that one day redeemed human beings will even judge angels. So, God's intent in creating us has very much to do with his own image and likeness. We were created to be like God and represent him. How are we as humans more like God than the rest of his creation? There are four implications to consider:

MORAL

Human beings are *morally* more like God. We have the ability to reason and the ability to use logic and the ability to learn. This sets us apart from the rest of creation. It's true that some animals display a remarkable ability to learn, and have remarkable cognitive capabilities. But there's a difference. Animals do not engage in abstract reasoning. You don't see animals writing the history of their kind. Animals do not get involved in art to display nature. Animals do not write literature. Animals are not involved in the explanation of philosophical concepts.

We've also been given an inner sense of the difference between right and wrong. Apostle Paul says that we have God's law written on our hearts. Isn't that interesting? People everywhere, for all time, have had an inner sense of the difference between things that are right and the things that are wrong because they were made in the image of God.

ACCOUNTABLE

All humans have an awareness of *accountability*. There is an innate understanding that we have been created and that we will have to give an account. This is a God consciousness that all people have. That's the reason there has never been found a group of human beings, ever, that does not worship.

All human beings worship.

People may pervert that worship to the worship of themselves, but all human beings worship. In us all, there is a God consciousness and also a desire to worship that God.

SPIRITUAL

Being made in the image of God has *spiritual* aspects. This means that we are not just physical bodies. Being made in the image of God means that the *real us* is immaterial. We are spirit beings. We have physical bodies for this world in which God has placed us, but the real us is immaterial. We have a spiritual life so that we can connect to God who is Spirit. *Our* spirit is able to connect to *his* Spirit. We have spiritual life and we have *immortal existence*. Because we are made in the image of God, we will live forever. A billion years from now each of us will still be alive.

**A billion years from now,
each of us will still be alive.**

RELATIONAL

There is also a *relational* aspect to being made in the image of God. There is something remarkable in Genesis 1:26. Let's look at it again. "Let us make man in our image, after our likeness." Who is the "us" and who is the "our?" This is God speaking and God says, "Us." This is the first hint in the Bible that within the one God there is a plurality of personalities. This is the first reference to the Trinity, which will be revealed throughout Scripture. God is one but he eternally exists in three persons—Father, Son, and the Holy Spirit—so that in God there is relationship. In God, there is actual, spiritual community.

That's an amazing thing to think about. By creating us in his image, God is allowing us to enter into the communion that exists between Father, Son, and Holy Spirit. We will never be equal to God, but being made in his likeness, according to his image, and being given spiritual existence, we are able to enter into a communion with God and all of his Persons. And we're able to do that together. That's ultimately what the body of Christ is all about. We as Christians, gather together in worship and our spirits, given to us by God, are communing with his Spirit in worship, and we are doing this together as the body of Christ. How amazing! When we think about God's intent in the creation of mankind, it should lead us to worship.

Let's consider what David wrote about his worship as he thought about himself and mankind in Psalm 8:3-6.

> When I look at your heavens, the work of
> your fingers,
>   the moon and the stars, which you have set in
> place,
> what is man that you are mindful of him,
>   and the son of man that you care for him?
> Yet you have made him a little lower than the
> heavenly beings
>   and crowned him with glory and honor.
> You have given him dominion over the works of
> your hands;
>   you have put all things under his feet,

David is thinking about this incredible, amazing truth that human beings are made in the image of God, and have been given dominion over the works of God's hands. This is *worshipful*, but the way that this becomes even more worshipful is when it becomes *personal*. When we take these foundational truths, and begin to make them personal, we find that not only is the whole of *mankind* made in the image of God, but *every individual* as well. *You* are made in the image of God.

> So God created man in his own image,
> in the image of God he created him;
> male and female he created them.
> (Genesis 1:27)

God created mankind, and he created mankind male and female. Both men and women are image bearers of God. But men and women are created distinctively. God says, "male and female he created them." Genesis 2:7 provides us with even more intimate details of the creation story involving the creation of man. We see in this verse how the creation of man becomes very personal and very individual. "…then the Lord God formed the man of dust from the ground and breathed into his nostrils the breath of life, and the man became a living creature."

There is such intentionality in this! We are given a picture in our minds of God on his knees scooping up some dirt and fashioning that dirt into the form of a man. Then notice the intimacy when Scripture says that God breathed into man's nostrils the breath of life. God is creating Adam and he is doing it *personally* and *individually*. He is breathing his own life into the body of this one human being. There is nothing *evolutionary* about this. There is no randomness. Nor is there an eon of time passing with particles joining together out of thin air. This is God Almighty individually and intimately involved in the creation of man. Man is created not in randomness, but with very real, personal intimacy. And the same intentionality occurs with the creation of the woman.

> Then the Lord God said, "It is not good that the
> man should be alone; I will make him a helper
> fit for him." [Not a servant but a counterpart, a
> companion.] Now out of the ground
> the Lord God had formed every beast of the
> field and every bird of the heavens and brought
> them to the man to see what he would call them.
> And whatever the man called every living
> creature, that was its name. The man gave
> names to all livestock and to the birds of the
> heavens and to every beast of the field. But for
> Adam there was not found a helper fit for
> him. So the Lord God caused a deep sleep to fall
> upon the man, and while he slept took one of his
> ribs and closed up its place with flesh. And the
> rib that the Lord God had taken from the man he
> made into a woman and brought her to the man.
> (Genesis 2:18-22)

Notice that God is *equally* creating both Adam and Eve. He uses the same basic materials. Even though a rib is taken from the man to make Eve, it's still the same basic material. God is uniquely creating the woman as a companion/counterpart to the man. Both are different and unique but both are God's image bearers. And when God brought the woman to the man, I'm sure Adam said resoundingly, "Viva La Difference!" Both male and female are God's image bearers, created distinctively by God, and they are created for that distinction.

> So God created man in his own image,
> in the image of God he created him;
> male and female he created them.
> (Genesis 1:27)

The difference between male and female is *God* determined. It is not *man* determined. Nor is it *self-* determined. It is God who appoints the very DNA of human beings. This assembling of DNA material is not *self-* determination, *man* determination, or *cultural* determination, but by *God's* determination.

Reflect for a moment about the importance of God's image. The image of God is so important to the Lord that he is very much concerned about protecting and respecting that image. Image bearers are to be respected and protected.

As a matter of fact, the first responsibility God gave human government was to protect his image. Genesis 9 details the account of Noah and his family leaving the Ark. God had destroyed the Earth because of mankind's wickedness, and then he made a covenant with mankind. The sign of that covenant is the rainbow and every time we see it we are reminded of the covenant that God has made with us.

It is important to keep in mind one of the responsibilities of that covenant God gave to mankind. "Whoever sheds the blood of man, by man shall his blood be shed, for God made man in his own image" (Genesis 9:6). God proclaims that the crime of murder is much more than the taking of a life. It is an assault on God himself because every human being is made in his image. God said that anyone guilty of deliberately murdering someone who is made in his image is also guilty of assaulting the very representation of God. The murderer's life is to be forfeited for that crime. That command is in the covenant that is represented by the rainbow. God wants human lives protected, and he wants those image bearers respected.

**God wants image bearers
protected and respected.**

In James 3:8-9, James said, "…no human being can tame the tongue. It is a restless evil, full of deadly poison. With it we bless our Lord and Father, and with it we curse people who are made in the likeness of God." The Lord does not take lightly, the defamation of other people's character. Nor does he take lightly malicious attacks on others because those "others" are other image bearers. They represent him. God's image is to be protected and it is to be respected.

Being an image bearer is where a true self-image and a true identity begin. As much as we hear about personal identity and self-image, we cannot fully understand self-image and personal identity apart from the truth that we are image bearers.

We are made in the image of God.

It is impossible to find our true identity in ourselves, by ourselves. It cannot be discovered through our own effort. Our identity comes from being made in God's image. It is found in the One who made us and in whose image we bear.

David leads us in wonder and worship in Psalm 139. If there were no other words in the Bible but these words, we would know what God says about life, even the life of the unborn. They are unborn, yes, but they have life. They are *already* image bearers. The Bible is replete with this honoring of life. Here we find David beautifully worshiping God, infinitely and intimately. "For you formed my inward parts; you knitted me together in my mother's womb"

(Psalm 139:13). This creation of life is not random and it is not by chance.

> For you formed my inward parts;
>   you knitted me together in my mother's womb.
> I praise you, for I am fearfully and wonderfully made.
> Wonderful are your works;
>   my soul knows it very well.
> My frame was not hidden from you,
> when I was being made in secret,
>   intricately woven in the depths of the earth. (Psalm 139:13-15)

David is talking about the forming of the human body in the dark place of the womb of the mother. Like the depths of the earth, there in the darkness, and even before the mother knows the child is there, God is weaving together the tissues and the structure of that body.

"Your eyes saw my unformed substance" (Psalm 139:16). "Unformed substance" is the Hebrew word that refers specifically to the human embryo. David is saying that God saw him and knew him in his embryonic state, and that even before he had a physical body, according to the mind of God, David was a living person. God saw him, and David continues "…in your book were written, every one of them, the days that were formed for me, when as yet there was none of them" (Psalm 139:16).

Every human being, as they are being formed in the womb and until the very moment of their death, has dignity, value, and worth as an image bearer. We are personally and lovingly created by God. *God created you.* Claiming this as truth is not arrogant or prideful. To say, "God created me," is the beginning of true wisdom.

God precisely created you.

God chose the unique characteristics that are a part of you. His sovereign plan and his purpose are wrapped up in the very characteristics of your body. And he purposefully created you. The Bible says that you were created for those days that were formed for you (Psalm 139:16).

The fact that we are made in the very image of God is an awesome and amazing thing. It gives us our identity and our personhood. To know that we are his image bearers gives us the understanding of the very purpose of our life. That image has been marred by sin, yes, but thank God, as we are going to see, there is One that has been sent from him. And this One has been made in God's image as well, the image of his Son. He has come to free us from the distorted image brought about by sin. We will focus on this glorious truth in the chapters that follow.

R.E.A.P. GUIDE

READ:

Genesis 1:26-31
Psalm 8

EXAMINE:

1. What did God teach you through *In His Image,* Chapter 1?
2. Psalm 8 describes our position as God's image bearers, even in the fallen world in which we now live. What should be our response to this privileged position (Psalm 8:1, 8:3-4, and 8:9)?
3. What are some ways that God has made men and women to be like him (Psalm 8:5-8)?
4. What is there to learn about God in both Genesis 1 and Psalm 8 that causes you to love and worship him?

APPLY:

- How should a proper understanding of the image of God change the way you think and act toward those individuals who are thought of as weak, insignificant or unattractive to the world?

PRAY:

- Praise God for creating you and those around you.
- Ask for grace to live faithfully as God's representative on Earth.

PART II: HIS IMAGE DISTORTED

2

Shattered Mirrors, Broken Dreams

My wife Susan and I were reminiscing recently about growing up in the mid-west and attending the county fairs. County fairs were a big deal. School would let out and we would enjoy the entire day with our friends, eating great food, experiencing fun rides and playing challenging games.

I especially remember the House of Mirrors. What a fantastic time we would have looking at our altered images. We would see the reflection of our friends in the mirror, make faces at each other and fall on the ground laughing. It was an amazing time. We would wind our way through the maze of images and sometimes get disoriented and lost. After a while, though, we would grow tired of the strange reflections. Quite frankly, I was glad when we got out of there and the experience was over.

But imagine, what if you couldn't get out? What if the reflected images just went on and on and on, and when you finally escaped, the larger world around you was still filled with the same distorted images? What if your image was permanently distorted and the whole world was populated with altered images! Some of you may be saying to yourselves, "I think I saw that episode of Rod Serling's *The Twilight Zone*." But let me tell you something, it *is* the real world we live in. According to the Bible, *we* are the distorted images.

In Genesis Chapter 1, the Bible tells us that we are made in God's image. Incredible! Amazing! It is overwhelming, yet true, that every human being is made in the image of God. But if that is true, and it is absolutely true, how has the image of God become so distorted? How can the billions and billions of people on this planet be so unlike the God we sing about in worship? How can we be so unlike the One whose image we bear? And perhaps the most important question: what can we do about it? The answer to the problem is found at the *source* of the problem, when the distortion began. Let's read in Genesis 3:1-15 how the image of God became so distorted in the image bearers:

Now the serpent was more crafty than any other beast of the field that the Lord God had made.

He said to the woman, "Did God actually say, 'You shall not eat of any tree in the garden'?" And the woman said to the serpent, "We may eat of the fruit of the trees in the garden, but God said, 'You shall not eat of the fruit of the tree that is in the midst of the garden, neither shall you touch it, lest you die.'" But the serpent said to the woman, "You will not surely die. For God knows that when you eat of it your eyes will be opened, and you will be like God, knowing good and evil." So when the woman saw that the tree was good for food, and that it was a delight to the eyes, and that the tree was to be desired to make one wise, she took of its fruit and ate, and she also gave some to her husband who was with her, and he ate. Then the eyes of both were opened, and they knew that they were naked. And they sewed fig leaves together and made themselves loincloths.

And they heard the sound of the Lord God walking in the garden in the cool of the day, and the man and his wife hid themselves from the presence of the Lord God among the trees of the garden. But the Lord God called to the man and said to him, "Where are you?" And he said, "I heard the sound of you in the garden, and I was afraid, because I was naked, and I hid myself." He said, "Who told you that you were naked? Have you eaten of the tree of which I commanded you not to eat?" The man said, "The woman whom you gave to be with me, she gave me fruit of the tree, and I ate." Then the Lord God said to the woman, "What is this that you have done?" The woman said, "The serpent deceived me, and I ate."

The Lord God said to the serpent,

"Because you have done this,
    cursed are you above all livestock
    and above all beasts of the field;
on your belly you shall go,
    and dust you shall eat
    all the days of your life.
I will put enmity between you and the woman,
    and between your offspring and her offspring;
he shall bruise your head,
    and you shall bruise his heel."
(Genesis 3:1-15)

This is how the world we live in became a House of Mirrors. Our very lives, originally designed to be God's image bearers, are filled with distorted images. How this impacts us and how we are able to overcome it, in some measure, is all included in this Genesis account, as this tragic story also contains the wonderful answer.

How was it possible that such a disaster could take place in paradise? How did it begin? It began by disrespecting God. God was *misrepresented,* if you will. And the misrepresentation was first made by the master of smoke and mirrors himself—Satan. In the story Satan takes the form of a snake. How appropriate is that?! He is called in the Bible, "The old serpent, the devil" (Revelation 12:9 & 20:2).

Satan is in the garden. Notice his cunning craftiness. He does not come to the image bearers, Adam and Eve, with a direct attack on God. He knows that will not work. Adam and Eve know God. They love God. So, Satan does not come to them with a direct assault on God. Instead he comes with a *question*. It's the first question recorded in the Bible. And the question is not just a question. There is a purpose behind the question. The question is an *insinuation*. It is a questioning of God's truthfulness, and an insinuation that God is not trustworthy.

"Now the serpent was more crafty than any other beast of the field that the Lord God had made. He said to the woman, "Did God actually say, 'You shall not eat of any tree in the garden?'" (Genesis 3:1). What is Satan's first assault on mankind? It is found in the cunning questioning of God's word. Satan put a question mark where God put a period.

Satan puts a question mark
where God puts a period.

God said, "You should not eat of this tree or you will die." And Satan said, "Did God actually say that?" Satan begins with a questioning of whether truth is absolute or relative. "Did God actually say this?" Next, Satan questions God's *motives*. Notice he quickly moves from questioning God's *truthfulness* to questioning God's *trustworthiness*. "But the serpent said to the woman, 'You will not surely die. For God knows that when you eat of it your eyes will be opened, and you will be like God, knowing good and evil'" (Geneses 3:4-5).

Do you notice the progression here? Satan begins by questioning the truthfulness of God, and then he questions not only God's message but God's motive as well. He questions God's heart. Satan puts doubt into Eve's mind. *"God is not really being honest with you, Eve."* And then Satan moves on to, *"God is really not good. Oh, I know, he shows himself to be good, and he seems good, but he's not really good because he knows something he doesn't want you to know. He is experiencing something he doesn't want you to experience. God's really holding back from you,*

26

Eve." And here is his hissing lie, *"God is greedy of his godhood and he doesn't want to share his godhood with you."*

What is Satan doing? He's speaking out of his own evil heart. After all, it was Satan who, eons earlier, said he would be like the Most High. And now he brings out of his own evil, this sinister lie, *"God is not really good. He's holding back. And if you will just go ahead and express your freedom, you will know what it's like to be God."* And Eve listened. There's a valuable lesson in this for us. Never listen to a snake, even if the snake has two legs. Never listen to a snake who questions the word of God.

Never listen to *any snake* who questions the word of God.

Eve listened. And then her response went a little further. Eve listened to Satan and then *she looked.* Eve is looking, but she is looking in the wrong direction. She's not looking to God. She begins looking elsewhere. She begins to change her focus from a focus on God, and who she is in God, and she begins to look at what is "supposedly" being withheld from her. Her focus becomes displaced.

Unfortunately, this is the next step downward. No sin has happened yet. Nothing has been violated, but there is a step taken in the wrong direction. Eve's focus becomes displaced.

So when the woman saw that the tree was good
for food, and that it was a delight to the eyes,
and that the tree was to be desired to make one
wise, she took of its fruit and ate, and she also
gave some to her husband who was with
her, and he ate. (Genesis 3:6)

Do you see the change of focus? Eve's focus moves from
her creator to the *created*. She changes where she's looking
from the creator, (the one who has made her in his image),
to the things that God has created.

Eve changed her focus from the *creator* to the *created*.

And then notice this; it's very subtle. Eve's focus
changes from her *liberty* to her *limitation*. She has complete
liberty. Any of the trees. Any of the fruit. Any of the
vegetation in all of its delightfulness. It's all hers. The
world is hers. Paradise is hers. Yet, she changes her focus
from all the liberty she has to the one limitation. That's
exactly where Satan wants her to focus. He doesn't want
her to think about her liberty. He wants her to focus on her
one limitation. Sound familiar?

The Bible says, "Eve saw" (Genesis 3:6). She intently
gazed at this fruit. She *saw* that it was good for food and it

was delightful to the eyes. Its promise was to make one wise. The more Eve focused on the fruit, the bigger and more luscious it grew in her mind. She became laser-focused on the very thing that was forbidden. God had said, "This one thing is off limits." And as she focused on it, it became even more desirable and more wonderful to her. This is the very definition of the beginning of lust. Not sexual lust but worldly desires, desiring what the Father has forbidden. The thing that is forbidden becomes the focus.

Temptation is when
the *forbidden* becomes our *focus*.

Apostle John wrote to Christians in the first century and also speaks to us today:

> "Do not love the world or the things in the
> world. If anyone loves the world, the love of the
> Father is not in him. For all that is in the
> world—the desires [lust] of the flesh and the
> desires [lust] of the eyes and pride of life—is
> not from the Father but is from the world"
> (1 John 2:15-16).

What was it that Eve focused on? She saw the fruit and that it was good for food. (The lust of the flesh.) She saw that it was delightful to the eyes. (The lust of the eyes.) And she desired to make herself wise. (The pride of life.)

Do you see what's being described here? An image bearer's focus is moving away from God and toward a focus on self. Her focus is not on liberty, but on the limitations and what is forbidden. It is the absorption with the self that is beginning to have an impact in Eve's heart. The building block of sin is selfishness. It is the very DNA of sin. Self-focused reasoning flows like this: *"You want this? You can have it. You can be more than you are. Set yourself free from those chains of religion that hold you back. Release yourself from all that legalistic teaching where some things are right and some things are wrong. You can grow and experience what it means to be your own person."* Does this sound familiar? Does this sound applicable to today's culture?

The building block of sin is selfishness.

Selfishness sells. This is how we sell cars today. This is how we sell cereal. This is how we explain to people how to find their career path. Selfishness. It is the DNA of sin. And it leads to a sinful betrayal. It led Eve to a disloyalty to God. The image bearer displaced her focus and it led to disloyalty. What brought such devastation? Look again at Genesis 3:6. Here's what happened:

So when the woman saw that the tree was good
for food, and that it was a delight to the eyes,
and that the tree was to be desired to make one
wise, she took of its fruit and ate, and she also
gave some to her husband who was with
her, and he ate. (Genesis 3:6)

Someone might ask, "That's it? A bite out of the apple and the whole world goes to hell? Really? And all that's wrong in the world flows out of this?!" No, it's not the bite out of the apple. It is the betrayal that's *in* the bite. It's the betrayal of God. It is the image bearers saying to the very One in whose image they had been made, "*We* will be the ones to decide what we do. You say no. We say yes."

The great tragedy is in the act of the betrayal. In betraying God, there is something Adam and Eve did not understand. They didn't understand that when they betrayed God they betrayed *themselves*. They thought they could eat of the forbidden fruit and it wouldn't have any effect on them. But they were made in the image of God, and in betraying God, they were betraying their very own identity.

**In betraying God,
we betray our own identity.**

What is the essence of sin? Rebellion. Treason. Sin is high treason against God. It's not a bite out of the apple. It's not just a little mistake. It is treason against our Heavenly Father. Therefore, sin is against ourselves. We betray ourselves who are made in God's image. We take a big swing at God and we smack ourselves in the face.

So, what actually happened to Adam and Eve? Outwardly, nothing actually happened. There was no lightning, no earthquake, no fire and brimstone. Adam and Eve still looked the same. As a matter of fact, their taste buds were probably singing the hallelujah chorus. But the juice of that fruit was the nectar of destruction because even though Adam and Eve looked the same, they weren't the same. And they knew it. In that moment, these living image bearers of life and beauty become living images of death and distortion.

They were still image bearers, yes, but immediately we discover cracks in the mirror. In the image that Adam and Eve reflected, there was now distortion. As we look at what happened to them, we must also look carefully at ourselves because our disloyalty to God causes the same thing—distortion.

Our disloyalty to God causes distortion.

So, what actually happened when Adam and Eve became disobedient? The image of God in them became distorted. We see this happen in four ways:

AVERSION

We first recognize the distortion in the *aversion*. Adam and Eve now have an aversion to God.

> And they heard the sound of the Lord God
> walking in the garden in the cool of the day, and
> the man and his wife hid themselves from the
> presence of the Lord God among the trees of the
> garden. But the Lord God called to the man and
> said to him, "Where are you?" (Genesis 3:8-9)

The same loving, good, and kind Father comes to his image bearers, but rather than running to him, as Adam and Eve always had before, they now hide from him. They hide from the very presence of the Lord. He calls out to them. *"Adam, where are you? Where are you, Eve?"* And they hide from their loving Father. Can you image hiding from the source of goodness and kindness of your life? Hiding from the One who has provided paradise for you? Hiding from the One who created you and made you in his image?

What a distortion! Adam and Eve were now hiding from the completely good and kind One.

So, what is it that disloyalty to God causes us to do? When we're disloyal to God, we have the desire to hide from him. The distortion causes us to forget his loving kindness and goodness because we can't bear to face his kindness and goodness, so we flee from him. We have an aversion to the intimacy we once shared with God. That's the first indication that the image bearers have had something terrible happen. Adam and Eve avoid God.

DIVERSION

The next thing that shows us that the image has been marred is the *diversion* that takes place. Adam and Eve divert responsibility. God said to them, "Who told you that you were naked? Have you eaten of the tree of which I commanded you not to eat?" The man replied, "The woman whom you gave to be with me, she gave me fruit of the tree, and I ate" (Genesis 3:11-12). Can you believe this? Adam is blame-shifting on his wife. But in reality, he's blame-shifting on God. *"If you hadn't given me this woman, my life wouldn't be so messed up. If you had not put this relationship here before me, everything would have been fine."* Then God confronted Eve, "What have you done?" And Eve blame-shifts, *"The serpent tempted me and I ate!"* (Genesis 3:13).

This took place thousands of years before the 1960's comedian, Flip Wilson, said, "The devil made me do it." But it's no joke. Blame-shifting image bearers divert responsibility by saying: "The devil made me do it. It's not my fault. It's the devil. Where did this devil come from, anyway? Who made the devil?" The result is that broken image bearers divert responsibility.

"My husband!" "My wife!" "My parents!" "The abuse that I suffered from my parents has ruined me forever, God, and you permitted it. I'm trashed for the rest of my life. I'm damaged goods." "My boss." "My job." Oh, and let's not forget this one, "The lousy government. It's the government that's ruining everything. How am I supposed to be the person God wants me to be when we have a government like ours? I mean, who can possibly pull off being a consistent image bearer when we live in such a messed-up world?!"

We refuse to look in the mirror. We refuse to look at our own image. And we don't want to come to God because we are afraid that in the beauty of God, we will be forced to see ourselves as we truly are—distorted image bearers.

SUBVERSION

Then there is the distortion of the image bearers impact on relationships. Relationships are ruined by *subversion*. Sin curses everything. The earth is cursed, there is a curse of pain and there is the curse in the toil of work. All these curses come out of this disloyalty and treason against God. But the curse isn't something *outside* of us. The curse is *inside* of us.

The curse is *inside* of us.

> To the woman he said,
> "I will surely multiply your pain in
> childbearing;
> > in pain you shall bring forth children.
> Your desire shall be contrary to your husband,
> > but he shall rule over you." (Genesis 3:16)

Those are not words of marriage and beauty. Those are words of the curse. "Your desire shall be contrary to your husband." *Desire* here means *a desire to control*. A desire to dominate. You will no longer have beauty and harmony in your relationship. Your desire will be to control your husband and he will rule over you. The word *rule* means *dictatorial rule*. This is not a formula for marriage, as some people seem to think. This is a result of the curse. And it's not just about marriage. It's about relationship. We have a natural desire to control and dominate people in any way possible.

This desire for control comes out of the curse.

PERVERSION

What is that desire for control doing? It's assuming the place of God. "Let me be in control. Let me decide what's going to happen. Ultimately it leads not just to aversion, and diversion, and subversion, but it ultimately leads to *perversion*—life away from Eden, life away from the presence of God, life away from the Lord of Glory. It is a terrible downward spiral. It becomes a life of hating those made in God's image. Let's take a look at Cain and see what was in his heart. "Cain spoke to Abel his brother. And when they were in the field, Cain rose up against his brother Abel and killed him" (Genesis 4:8). Cain murdered his brother. He murdered his fellow image bearer. Life away from Eden and the presence of God is a downward spiral. It's not *evolution*. This is not what the Bible is explaining here. It's *devolution*. The movement is downward. And what an awful spiral spin it is.

In Romans, apostle Paul perfectly describes what life is like away from Eden and away from God. It's the devolution of mankind and the image bearers. "For the wrath of God is revealed from heaven against all ungodliness and unrighteousness of men, who by their unrighteousness suppress the truth" (Romans 1:18).

Where did this downward spiral start? Remember? It started with an insinuating question, "Has God actually said...?" It started with suppressing the truth. What happens when truth is suppressed? Truth is suppressed for the purpose of unrighteousness. In Romans 1:19-32, Paul says that when truth is suppressed, it is suppressed with the goal of unrighteousness living.

PEOPLE GENERALLY

> For what can be known about God is plain to them, because God has shown it to them. For his invisible attributes, namely, his eternal power and divine nature, have been clearly perceived, ever since the creation of the world, in the things that have been made. So they are without excuse. For although they knew God, they did not honor him as God or give thanks to him, but they became futile in their thinking, and their foolish hearts were darkened. Claiming to be wise, they became fools, and exchanged the glory of the immortal God for images resembling mortal man and birds and animals and creeping things.
>
> Therefore God gave them up in the lusts of their hearts to impurity, to the dishonoring of their

bodies among themselves, because they
exchanged the truth about God for a lie [They
didn't want the truth. They wanted a lie.] and
worshiped and served the creature rather than
the Creator, who is blessed forever! Amen.

For this reason God gave them up
to dishonorable passions. For their women
exchanged natural relations for those that are
contrary to nature; and the men likewise gave up
natural relations with women and were
consumed with passion for one another, men
committing shameless acts with men and
receiving in themselves the due penalty for their
error.

And since they did not see fit to acknowledge
God, God gave them up to a debased mind to
do what ought not to be done. They were filled
with all manner of unrighteousness, evil,
covetousness, malice. They are full of envy,
murder, strife, deceit, maliciousness. They are
gossips, slanderers, haters of God, insolent,
haughty, boastful, inventors of evil, disobedient
to parents, foolish, faithless, heartless,
ruthless. Though they know God's righteous
decree that those who practice such

things deserve to die, they not only do them
but give approval to those who practice them.
(Romans 1:19-32)

All of that, the exchanging of truth for evil, has come to us today where we see millions of people march to glorify and to demand rights for these very debased activities. This is how far our culture has drifted. And the problem is not just *outside* of us. It's *inside* of us. As individuals.

PEOPLE INDIVIDUALLY

…as it is written:

"None is righteous, no, not one; no one
understands; no one seeks for God.
All have turned aside; together they have
become worthless;
   no one does good,
   not even one."
"Their throat is an open grave;
   they use their tongues to deceive."
"The venom of asps is under their lips."
"Their mouth is full of curses and bitterness."
"Their feet are swift to shed blood;
   in their paths are ruin and misery,
and the way of peace they have not known."

40

"There is no fear of God before their eyes."
(Romans 3:10-18)

Distorted image bearers, *in general,* are described in Romans 1, and the *individual* image bearer is described here, in Romans 3. This is man in the mirror, the new reflection of the image bearer. So terribly distorted! Sadly, as I read these verses, I see way too much of my own reflection in these words. How about you? As if this news wasn't bad enough. The really bad news is this—you can't fix it. You cannot fix this distorted image.

But here's the good news—you don't have to. We have been promised a Redeemer. In our text, which we will cover more completely in the next chapter, we receive the very first promise in the Bible. It is the promise made in the midst of all the distortion and sin. God said he would send a deliverer, and he will crush the enemy's head. (Genesis 3:15) And thank God that deliverer has come! And the deliverer is not man's pursuit of enlightenment. The deliverer is not more education. The deliverer is not more government. The deliverer is God himself in the form of Christ Jesus. He is able to deliver us. Why? Because as terrible as all this sin is, the Bible says, "...but where sin increased, grace abounded all the more..." (Romans 5:20).

There is grace from God in his Son Jesus Christ, and his grace is greater than all of our sins. You may be guilty of every sin that Paul has just described but your sin is not more powerful than the grace of God in Christ. And the Deliverer does not just cover your sin. He changes your heart. Jesus is the answer for us, and for everyone in this world. The promised Deliverer is Jesus Christ.

R.E.A.P. GUIDE

READ:

Genesis 3:1-24

EXAMINE:

1. What did God teach you through *In His Image,* Chapter 2?
2. What particular lie does the serpent say to Eve that undermines her and Adam as God's unique image bearers (Genesis 3:5)?
3. What are ways in which the snake attacks the goodness of God in Genesis 3:5?
4. Referring to the following verses, what ways was the image of God marred in man because of sin? (Genesis 3:8-10, Genesis 3:12, 16, & Genesis 3:17-19)
5. How did God plan to respond to the damage sin had brought upon his image bearers (Genesis 3:15)?

APPLY:

- *How can God be good and not give me everything I think I need to be happy?* When thoughts like these pop into your head this week, how will you choose to respond using God's word?

PRAY:

- Spend some time in private prayer, asking the Holy Spirit to reveal any sins to you so you can confess them and once again experience God's forgiveness and mercy (1 John 1:8-10).
- Leaders, guide the members of your group in a time of prayer, confessing their dependence on God's continued work of restoration in each of them into his image.
- Spend time praising God for his plan through Jesus to crush the serpent and begin the certain work of redemption in his people.

PART III: HIS IMAGE REDEEMED

3

A STORY OF TREES

T he every day, small things of life, can only be truly understood when held up to the light of a bigger truth. And there can be no bigger truth that encompasses our lives than the recognition that we were made in the image of God. We are his image bearers. And the knowledge of being made in the image of God and restored to his image, is the key that opens up the word of God. This awareness allows us a deeper and more thorough understanding of God's great plan, and how we fit into that plan.

One of the most sacred holidays in Israel is called the *Day of Remembrance*. It is set aside as a special day because it was on that date, January 27, 1945, that the survivors of the death camp at Auschwitz were liberated. The *Day of Remembrance* is a very solemn day for the nation of Israel. Special programs on television remind viewers how hideous it all truly was. Within a period of less than six years, six million Jewish people were exterminated by the demonically fueled hatred of antisemitism in the heart of the leaders of Nazism. The evil perpetrated on the Jews throughout the Holocaust was without precedence.

An amazing thing happened immediately after the liberation of those death camps. Though most of the Jewish population of Eastern and Western Europe had been exterminated, groups of the remaining Jews began to search for a place to settle. It is difficult to acknowledge but no country in Europe seemed willing to open their hearts for a resettlement of the Jews. In reality, and I believe providentially, many of those Jewish survivors did not think that they should remain there.

Some of them decided to return to their true homeland. By every kind of vessel and every type of transportation, hundreds began to make their way to Palestine, as it was called then. Upon arrival, they were immediately attacked, but they would not quit. It's an incredible story how they dwelt in caves and underground bunkers by day, and would only come out at night to sow their fields. They had a few weapons, but as more were brought to them, they began to fight back. And as they fought back, their existence became a little more secure.

They were under relentless attack but finally in May of 1948 that small group of Jewish people, in victory and in recognition, (led in great part by the United States and our

President, Harry Truman), was recognized as the sovereign state of Israel. From that time forward, thousands have made the journey back to their homeland and generations have been raised up. Approximately four million Jewish people reside there today. In 2016, for the first time in modern history, there were more Jews living in Israel than there were living in the United States.

When those early Jewish people returned to their promised land, the land promised to their ancestor Abraham, they discovered that during this time of persecution, their homeland had been completely denuded of all trees. So, they began to plant them. Since 1948, nearly 400 million trees have been planted in Israel in order to return it to a country of forests as it was in biblical times. Those trees are restoring physical health to the land and to the environment, helping to establish sustainable life in that part of the world. Every tree is a symbol of the hearts of those people who returned, and their descendants, resounding clearly, "We are planted here, and the nation will flourish even as these trees flourish!"

When you read biblical prophecy, these trees have significance. The Bible tells us that in the last days, the people of Israel will once again come to live in their homeland as a nation. Those replanted trees are symbols of restoration and hope, and symbols of a reclaiming of the promises that were made by God to Abraham.

We learn in Genesis 3 of a terrible distortion in the

Garden of Eden. Adam and Eve, the children of God, are ruined as image bearers. But in the midst of that ruin, there is a promise given—a promise of *restoration* and *redemption*. This story really is a story about trees. Let's take a look at Genesis 3:8-24:

> And they heard the sound of the Lord God
> walking in the garden in the cool of the day, and
> the man and his wife hid themselves from the
> presence of the Lord God among the trees of the
> garden. But the Lord God called to the man and
> said to him, "Where are you?" And he said, "I
> heard the sound of you in the garden, and I was
> afraid, because I was naked, and I hid myself."
> He said, "Who told you that you were naked?
> Have you eaten of the tree of which I
> commanded you not to eat?" The man
> said, "The woman whom you gave to be with
> me, she gave me fruit of the tree, and I ate."
> Then the Lord God said to the woman, "What is
> this that you have done?" The woman
> said, "The serpent deceived me, and I ate."
> The Lord God said to the serpent,
>
> "Because you have done this,
>   cursed are you above all livestock
>   and above all beasts of the field;
> on your belly you shall go,

and dust you shall eat
all the days of your life.
I will put enmity between you and the woman,
and between your offspring and her offspring;
he shall bruise your head,
and you shall bruise his heel."

To the woman he said,

"I will surely multiply your pain in childbearing;
in pain you shall bring forth children.
Your desire shall be contrary to your husband,
but he shall rule over you."

And to Adam he said,

"Because you have listened to the voice of your
wife
and have eaten of the tree
of which I commanded you,
'You shall not eat of it,'
cursed is the ground because of you;
in pain you shall eat of it all the days of your
life;
thorns and thistles it shall bring forth for you;
and you shall eat the plants of the field.
By the sweat of your face
you shall eat bread,

till you return to the ground,
　　for out of it you were taken;
for you are dust,
　　and to dust you shall return."

The man called his wife's name Eve, because she was the mother of all living. And the Lord God made for Adam and for his wife garments of skins and clothed them.

Then the Lord God said, "Behold, the man has become like one of us in knowing good and evil. Now, lest he reach out his hand and take also of the tree of life and eat, and live forever—" therefore the Lord God sent him out from the garden of Eden to work the ground from which he was taken. He drove out the man, and at the east of the garden of Eden he placed the cherubim and a flaming sword that turned every way to guard the way to the tree of life. (Genesis 3:8-24)

The *ruin* and the *restoration* of the relationship between Adam and Eve and God is crafted around a story of trees. There were many beautiful trees in the Garden of Eden but our attention is drawn to two in particular—*the*

Tree of Life and *the Tree of the Knowledge of Good and Evil.*

> And the Lord God planted a garden in Eden, in the east, and there he put the man whom he had formed. And out of the ground the Lord God made to spring up every tree that is pleasant to the sight and good for food. *The tree of life* was in the midst of the garden, and *the tree of the knowledge of good and evil.* (Genesis 2:8-9)

These two trees are *literal* trees. They did exist. And it's clear that they also had *spiritual significance.* Our attention is drawn to them because there is spiritual significance in them being placed in the garden.

One of them is called the Tree of Life, and we can imagine how beautiful that Tree of Life must have been. How delicious the fruit must have tasted! It was nothing like asparagus and turnips, and those other terrible vegetables that sprung up after the fall! The fruit on the Tree of Life was luscious fruit. The tree itself represented all that *is* life. It was the representation of life itself. This tree was a visible expression of the goodness of God who created all things. All the world working in perfect harmony—God and man and his creation. It's perfect. And in the middle of it all was this incredible tree that symbolized the goodness and beauty of God, and the sweetness of life lived with him. Adam and Eve lived with God in perfect joy and peace, delighting in him, and he, delighting in them.

The only requirement for Adam and Eve to continue to enjoy what God had given them, was to love and trust him. They needed only to maintain a loving loyalty to God and to give God their trust. That requirement was expressed in the second tree—the Tree of the Knowledge of Good and Evil. This tree represented God's goodness, his perfect will, his incredible kindness, and his purposes, which are wonderful. This tree is called the Tree of the Knowledge of *Good and Evil*—good, which is God's will, and evil, which is God's warning. The tree was a warning to Adam and Eve that evil existed.

Evil exists.

We know from Scripture that Evil existed for eons before the fall, when the most beautiful of all God's creatures, Lucifer, the leader of the angels, was lifted up in pride and desired to be like God. He led a rebellion against God but was defeated and cast out of heaven along with all the angels that rebelled along with him. (Ezekiel 28:12-19 & Isaiah 14:12-14.) Evil still exists. Lucifer is evil personified. God says that to know evil is to know death. To know evil, to rebel as Satan has rebelled, is to know death. That's the reason God warned Adam and Eve in

Genesis 2:17, "…but of the Tree of the Knowledge of Good and Evil you shall not eat, for in the day that you eat of it you shall surely die." This is God's warning of the tree of death, *"If you are disloyal, if you choose evil over good, if you follow the evil one instead of me, you will experience death."*

Adam and Eve were not created as robots. They were not programmed to do only what God wanted them to do. They were created in his image. They represented God. They had the ability to make choices. They had the ability to deliberate. They had the ability to make moral decisions. And God, in creating someone like himself, male and female, created in them the ability to make moral choices. And they chose evil.

How did that happen? How could their thinking be so twisted to actually choose evil? They chose evil because of the manner in which it was presented to them. Evil was not presented to Adam and Eve as terrible and awful and dark and hellish, but instead as something beautiful and worthy of desire. They chose evil because it was not presented to them truthfully, but instead, terribly misconstrued. Satan knew how to present evil.

Satan knows how to present evil.

This is not a serpent. This is the being of Satan, *using* the serpent. "But the serpent said to the woman, 'You will not surely die. For God knows that when you eat of it your eyes will be opened, and you will be like God, knowing good and evil'" (Genesis 3:4-5). Notice what this evil one is doing. Satan is putting questions into the minds of the image bearers about God's truthfulness. *"Did God actually say that you could not eat of this tree? Did God actually say that?"* Do you see how crafty Satan is? He is putting a question mark where God put a period.

Satan puts a question mark
where God puts a period.

Satan is questioning absolute truth. He's questioning whether there is a source for absolute truth. Satan is saying to Adam and Eve, *"Can you not determine your own truth? Aren't you image bearers able to decide for yourselves?"*

Satan then questions God's trustworthiness. He says to them, *"Let me tell you what's going on here. God is telling you not to eat of this fruit because he knows when you do, you will become like him. You will know good from evil. God is holding back on you. God doesn't want you to be all you can be. God is restricting you. God wants you to stay under his control. God doesn't want you to be fully independent. He doesn't want you experiencing true freedom like he has."* And tragically Adam and Eve believed the serpent and they betrayed their Father. They sinned. They disobeyed. They became disloyal. They rebelled against their all loving Father God.

What they didn't know was that by betraying their Father, they were betraying themselves because they were made in the image of the Father. So, in destroying the relationship they had with the Father, in choosing to go their own way, they were actually destroying themselves. By trying to liberate themselves from God, they ruined themselves in the process. They ruined their relationship with their Creator. Now they're hiding from him when they use to go running to him. God's voice use to be the delight of their ears. And now they're covering themselves and hiding from him.

In this act of disobedience, Adam and Eve also ruined their relationship with creation. Everything created by God now worked *against* them, not *with* them. They also destroyed the relationship they had with each other. They no longer looked at each other the same way. They're now ashamed of themselves. They're ashamed of each other. They're now blame-shifting on each other and trying to control one another. The beautiful and perfect relationship God had blessed them with was destroyed. The curse came and paradise was lost.

The curse came and paradise was lost.

Then the Lord God said, "Behold, the man has become like one of us in knowing good and evil. Now, lest he reach out his hand and take also of the tree of life and eat, and live forever—" therefore the Lord God sent him out from the garden of Eden to work the ground from which he was taken. He drove out the man, and at the east of the garden of Eden he placed the *cherubim* and a flaming sword that turned every way to guard the way to the tree of life. (Genesis 3:22-24)

Cherubim are guardian angels who guard the presence of God, his holiness, and his throne. After the fall, God placed cherubim at the east of the garden, along with a flaming sword that turned every direction to guard the way to the Tree of Life. The image bearers, Adam and Eve, were ruined and because of this, God banished them from the garden. But the most important element to remember from this Scripture is God's enormous grace shown in this single act.

God is not behaving as a bully by placing Adam and Eve out of the garden. He's not acting in anger that has totally consumed him. God knew beforehand what was going to happen. He's acting graciously because if Adam and Eve were to eat of the fruit of the Tree of Life in their fallen condition, they would be forced to live forever in that condemned condition. They would never be able to be changed. They would become like Satan himself who is beyond redemption, beyond hope, beyond repentance, and beyond restoration. Adam and Eve would be forced to live forever away from God's grace. So, in order to avoid this unending condemnation, God says to the cherubim, "Do not let them come back."

As God sees what Adam and Eve have done, he makes a pronouncement of curses. "You've cursed everything. You've cursed the earth. You've cursed yourselves. You've cursed your relationship." But in the midst of those curses, God also makes his first promise. If we look closely, we discover the first and only gleam of light in this dark story of ruined image bearers. Here's the first gospel promise in the Bible. God is speaking to the serpent in Genesis 3:15:

> "I will put enmity between you and the woman,
>   and between your offspring and her offspring;
> he shall bruise your head,
>   and you shall bruise his heel."

God says there will be descendants or followers of the serpent, and they will hate the descendants or followers of the faith of Adam and Eve. God is describing a spiritual conflict, but he's also talking about two individuals. He says to Satan, "I am going to put enmity between you and your offspring, and the woman and her offspring," and then God declares, "He will crush your head and you will bruise his heel. There is someone who is coming, Satan, who is going to crush you and all you stand for, and in crushing you, you will bruise his heel."

Now, where would this happen? It would happen on a *tree*. On the tree of Calvary to which Jesus was nailed. "Cursed is everyone who is hanged on a tree" (Galatians 3:13). For Jesus, it was the tree of death. Crucifixion. A horrible, torturous death. But what was so terrible about the cross, is not so much what *sort* of death took place there, but *whose* death it was. The Lord of Glory was nailed to the tree of death. The Prince of life. The second Adam from God. The perfect image bearer and Son of God. And…his heel was bruised. When the Son of God was hanged on that tree, the spikes that were driven through his feet bruised his heel.

But Jesus was not a victim. He was a victor. Because as he was suffering and dying for sinners on that cross, his heel was not just being bruised by the spikes. His heel was being bruised because in that moment he was crushing the head of Satan. He was conquering the power of Satan. Jesus was the Image Bearer, perfectly devoted to the Father's will. He would not go astray. He would not disobey as Adam and Eve did in eating of the fruit of the Tree of the Knowledge of Good and Evil. Jesus would only desire the knowledge of God to fulfill His Father's will, even to the point of death. In doing so, Jesus would make the cross, the hideous tree of death, into the glorious tree of eternal life. And in his loving death, the Prince of Life would crush the head of the serpent, the prince of death.

Jesus crushed the head of the serpent.

Now, do you remember what God placed outside the garden so that nobody could come back in and eat of the Tree of Life? If anyone ate of the Tree of Life in their fallen sinful condition, they would be cursed forever. What did God put there for their protection? For our protection? The *cherubim.*

When Jesus died on the cross, a huge curtain in the temple separated the holy sanctuary from a chamber called the Holy of Holies. Behind that curtain rested the Ark of the Covenant containing the Ten Commandments engraved on tablets of stone. On top of the Ark was the beautiful throne of God called the Mercy Seat, where it was believed God dwelt with his people. Once a year sacrifices of blood were applied over the top of that Mercy Seat and God would consider the sins of the people covered by that blood, forgiven.

The curtain that hung in front of the Ark of the Covenant, from the top of the temple to the bottom, had something woven on it. Do you remember what it was? It was the flaming *cherubim*. Flaming cherubim were woven into the fabric of that curtain, in effect saying, "Stay out. You cannot come as a sinner into the presence of Holy God and live."

As Jesus was dying, with his final strength he cried out, "It is finished!" (John 19:30). It was a victor's cry. Jesus had lived the perfect life as God's Image Bearer. He had given up his life as a substitute for image bearers who had sinned against God. He had conquered Satan by his perfect life, and by his atoning death. When Jesus cried out, "It is finished," the Bible says that the curtain in that temple was torn from top to bottom. What did the tearing of that curtain mean? It meant, *"Come back. You can come back now because my Son has made the way. My Son has crushed the serpent's head. He has been bruised, but he has paid the price for you and the door is open. All of you sons and daughters of Adam and Eve, all you sinners, as broken as you are, you can come back now through my Son, Jesus."*

R.E.A.P. GUIDE

READ:

Genesis 3:15
1 Corinthians 15:1-7, 20-34, 49
Colossians 1:15
2 Corinthians 3:12-18
Romans 8:28-29

EXAMINE:

1. What truth stood out to you from *In His Image,* Chapter 3?

2. 1 Corinthians 15:1-7 describes the work of Jesus on the cross and his absolute power in resurrection (1 Corinthians 15:20-28). Christ's resurrection is the certain hope that believers will have the image of God restored to them (1 Corinthians 15:49). What commands does Paul give Christians in light of these truths (1 Corinthians 15:31-34 and 15:58)?

3. Christ is restoring the image of God in us, as his people, each day we live. According to 2

Corinthians 3:12-18, how do we begin to reflect the image of God in our lives (2 Corinthians 3:18)?

4. Colossians 3:1-10 describes this process of the daily restoration of God's image in his people. In light of all Christ has accomplished on our behalf, what does Paul say is the believer's responsibility?

APPLY:

- It is said that we become like the individuals we spend time with, watch, and want to be like. What influences in your life are drawing you away from becoming like the Lord Jesus Christ?
- In your daily life, what are some ways you could spend time with, watch, and become more like Jesus?
- Commit to one thing you will do in the coming weeks to regularly spend time with the Lord.

PRAY:

- As you talk to God in prayer, thank Jesus for all he has done to restore you to God and to restore the image of God in you.
- Ask the Holy Spirit to reveal any areas of your life that are habitually leading you away from Jesus.
- As you read the Bible, ask the Holy Spirit to reveal

to you the glories of Jesus Christ, the perfect image bearer of God, and to help you worship him.

4

THE TREE OF CALVARY

B eing made in God's image is central to our identity.
Apart from understanding what it means to be made
in his image, we cannot understand who we are or
what we are supposed to be. But we also cannot understand
the gospel unless we are able to see clearly that the gospel
is all about the Lord restoring and redeeming people to his
image. Christ's message is about restoring and redeeming
image bearers to the purpose for which God created them.

In 1973 in northwest Ohio, there was an unknown but
very active satanic cult. Part of the initiation into this cult
was for people to profane some sacred object. They needed
to destroy something that was identified with Christ. There
was a young man who desired entrance into this group and
the right of admission for him was to burn down a church.

He chose a place of worship that was located on the
outskirts of the county. One night, with several gallons of

gasoline, he broke into the sanctuary, poured the gas all over the platform, the pews, around the building, and then set the church on fire. The flames were seen from the nearby Interstate 75, but before the emergency response team could get there, the entire building was engulfed in flames.

It was determined that arson was the cause and was eventually connected back to the satanic cult. Because of the circumstances, the pastor of the church was often in the news reminding the people that God's church was not bricks, mortar or wood, but that God's church was people. The pastor wanted the community to know that their church was very much alive and well. When the congregation pledged themselves to rebuild the church, the pastor said to them, "Watch God work." He would repeat the statement on television and radio so that the community would understand.

Watch God work.

By God's grace, that church was able to not only rebuild, but to rebuild much larger than it had ever been before. And because of the notoriety of what had happened, many people were drawn to attend the services, and scores and scores of people were saved. An incredible revival broke out, which was an amazing work of the Lord. That church was Calvary Baptist Church in Findlay, Ohio. For seven years, my wife Susan and I were blessed to be a part of that church and serve on their staff. We came to the Calvary Baptist a few years after these events took place, and it was a wonderful blessing to work with a congregation of people and a community where God had literally given *beauty* in exchange for *ashes*. God brought about redemption and he was using the attack of the enemy to do it. That's how God works.

That's the good news of the gospel. Even though the image of God in us has been marred and ruined by sin, there is a God whose grace is greater. Out of that ruin, God brings restoration and redemption. And he uses hatred and the attack of the enemy to do it. There is no denying—we serve a great God.

Genesis 2:17 reads, "but of the tree of the knowledge of good and evil you shall not eat, for in the day that you eat of it you shall surely die." In other words, if you disobey God, if you rebel, if you follow the way of Satan, you will die. So, the Tree of the Knowledge of Good and Evil became a tree of death. God had set before Adam and Eve the choice of *life* and *death.* The choice of *life* meant that they could enjoy God, have fellowship with him, accept his love, and respond in love to him. But there was also for them, the choice of *death*. They were not robots. They were made in the image of God. They had the ability to make moral choices. They *could* choose death. They *could* choose evil. And Satan knew that.

Satan knows we have a choice.

Tragically, Adam and Eve heard the lie of the serpent, and they believed the serpent rather than their Father. They believed the serpent when he questioned God's trustworthiness. The serpent questioned God's intent for Adam and Eve. And so, they betrayed their Father, and in betraying their Father, they betrayed themselves. They were made in the image of God, and since they were made in the image of God, to betray their Father meant bringing ruin upon themselves. Adam and Eve disobeyed God that day and the curse of sin came. Death came. Not an immediate, physical death, but a spiritual death came over them.

Let's not overlook what God did. God extended his tender mercy to Adam and Eve. Now lest they eat of this fruit and live eternally in this hopeless fallen condition, lest they eat of the tree of the fruit of life and live doomed and damned, never able to change, God barred the way back into the garden with a flaming sword and the cherubim. Then, even as God was pronouncing a curse on Satan who had brought evil and temptation to mankind, God made the first promise of the Bible. That promise, made in Genesis 3:15, is the first reference to the gospel and to his Son, Jesus.

"I will put enmity between you and the woman,
    and between your offspring and her offspring;
he shall bruise your head,
    and you shall bruise his heel."

In the midst of the wreck and ruin in the garden of Eden, and also in the image bearers themselves, God promises to send someone to the rescue. This someone will be of the offspring of the woman, and will crush the head of Satan, and in doing so, his heel will be bruised. He will be wounded, but in his wounding, he will accomplish the victory of God. And this wounding and this victory will take place on another tree—the tree of Calvary.

The tree of Calvary is also a tree of death. A hideous death, yes. A terrible death. But it's not what *kind* of death that is paramount, but *whose* death it was. It was the death of the Lord of glory. It was the death of the Son of God. It was the death of the Prince of Life. It was the death of the Second Adam. The second Image Bearer from God. It was *his* death. He was the one who was of the seed of the woman, virgin born, and he would be the one who would be wounded on the cross. But notice, in his wounding what he would do. What was the promise? "He will crush your head. He will be a victor. He will conquer." And that is what happened at Calvary. On the cross, in his perfect obedience as the Second Adam, the Lord Jesus Christ destroyed the power of the enemy. He crushed the head of Satan. And Jesus, in his resurrection, triumphed over him.

The tree of Calvary is the tree of death that becomes the tree of life because victory was accomplished there. And the victory is for us—the image bearers. Our ultimate problem is that we are cursed by sin. And how can we possibly be delivered from this curse? By Jesus. But how does Jesus on the tree deliver us from this curse? Galatians 3:13 states clearly, "Christ redeemed us from the curse of the law *by becoming a curse* for us—for it is written, 'Cursed is everyone who is hanged on a tree'"—

Christ redeemed us. That word redeemed means to purchase. Christ has purchased us to free us from the curse. How does he do it? He does it by becoming accursed himself. He becomes the accursed one. And on that cross, which is the cross of his death, he takes *our* curse, so that the tree of death *for him* becomes the tree of life *for us*. The cross becomes the tree of life because Jesus took our curse from us and put it on himself.

But the tree of Calvary is also the tree of life because of what Jesus gave to us. If you think of the cross as Jesus taking our sins on himself, you're absolutely right, but you're only half right. The tree of life is not just about Jesus taking on our sins. What Jesus did for us on the cross also involves our Savior placing his righteousness onto us.

In 2 Corinthians 5:21, apostle Paul says, "For our sake he made him to be sin who knew no sin, so that in him we might become the righteousness of God." Jesus took upon himself, what we are—*sin*, so he could give to us that what he is—*righteousness*.

The cross is the tree of life because on this cross there is good—Jesus, the altogether Good One. But also on the cross is evil. It's a tree of good and evil just as in the Garden of Eden. The greatest evil that the world has ever known is the crucifixion of Jesus Christ. The evil of our sin has been placed on the Good One. My sin is there on the cross. On the cross is perfect goodness—the righteousness of God in Christ, and on the cross is evil—my sin. The Bible says that my sin is placed on Jesus. He became my sin so that on the tree, his righteousness might be placed on me.

It's the *great exchange*—my sin is placed on Jesus, and Jesus' righteousness is placed on me. That is the reason the cross is the tree of life because it is the tree of good *and* evil—the goodness of God in Christ, and the evil of my sin rebelling against God. My sin is placed on the perfect image bearer Jesus, the second Adam, and the righteousness of the perfect image bearer is placed to my account.

Maybe as you read this, you're realizing that this cross is not *your* tree of life. And you're wondering what it would take to make this truth about what Jesus did on the cross, become the gospel truth for you. How do you find true salvation like that experienced by Christians you know? The Bible says this happens through repentance and faith. The Bible says I must repent of my sin. Notice I write "repentance" not "do penance." Doing "penance" is not repentance. Doing "penance" means trying to do something to earn God's mercy, and God's mercy cannot be earned. Repentance is the changing of your mind, which causes a change in direction. It means literally *to change your mind*. You realize that you're going the wrong way so you change your direction. You turn toward God. You may be thinking, "M*y sin is wrong and I want to turn to God*." Repentance is when you actually turn away from your sin and then turn yourself toward God.

What do I repent about? I repent about what my sin *is*. My sin is rebellion and treason against God. My sin is no different than the sin of Adam and Eve. It is rebellion and treason against the God who gave us life. I repent because of what my sin is—it's against God. And I repent because of what my sin has done. What has my sin done?

Jesus died because of your sin. So often we say this, and it is absolutely true. Praise God. Jesus died for our sin. But I want you to know something. He also died *because* of your sin. You and I are guilty of the death of the Son of God. I am not neutral. You are not neutral. Jesus Christ died because of you. And until you are born again, you are guilty of the death of the Son of God. It is not neutrality. It is not, "You might be okay. You're going to do better." If you are not born again, you are guilty of the death of Jesus. You and I are guilty of deicide. Our sins put Jesus on that cross. We have killed the Lord of Glory. Until that grips you, you are a billion miles away from the Kingdom of God. Do not deceive yourself. Until you understand that you are guilty of the death of Jesus, you will not repent.

Repenting of your sins is repenting of your rebellion against God. What did your rebellion do? It caused the death of the Son of God. How can the cross become a tree of life for you? Because of God's mercy, the cross becomes the tree of life when you repent and place your faith in the One who died for you. You caused his death. I caused his death. But in the incredible, amazing, Providence of God, he died for the people who caused his death. He died for the very ones who nailed him to the tree. And it was our sin, not the Roman nails, that held him there.

Jesus died for us.

Salvation is when we have faith in Jesus who suffered and died for us. Faith is knowing that he is my substitute and my Savior. On the cross, Jesus became what I am. He received what I deserve. He became what I am—sin. And he received what I deserve—death and separation from God. He's my *substitute* but he's also my *Savior*. Isn't it amazing? I become what he is and receive what he deserves. 2 Corinthians 5:21 reads, "For our sake he made him to be sin who knew no sin, so that in him we might become the righteousness of God." Jesus became what I am and received what I deserve, so I can become what he is and receive what he deserved. That happens for you when you repent of your sins and place your faith in Jesus Christ. And it happens through faith.

In Romans 3:20, apostle Paul addresses what penance and works cannot do:

> For by works of the law no human being will be
> justified in his sight, since through the law
> comes knowledge of sin.

The law of God, the standard of God, cannot save you. Not because there is something wrong with the *law*. The problem is there is something wrong with *us*. The law is the mirror. The law can show you that your face is dirty, but the law cannot wash it. It just shows us. The law provides for us the knowledge of our sins and the truth that we have fallen short of what God requires. Paul continues in Romans 3:21-24:

> But now the righteousness of God has been
> manifested apart from the law, although the Law
> and the Prophets bear witness to it—the
> righteousness of God through faith in Jesus
> Christ for all who believe. For there is no
> distinction: for all have sinned and fall short of
> the glory of God, and are justified by his grace

as a gift, through the redemption that is in Christ Jesus…

What *can* save you is the righteousness of God that comes through faith in Jesus Christ for all who believe. When a person has faith in Jesus, they are given the righteousness of God. The apostle Paul refers to this truth two times. This passage is the very spark of the Reformation. These verses turned on the light in the midst of the darkness in the religion of medieval times. A Roman Catholic Augustinian monk by the name of Martin Luther was trying to earn favor with God. He was struggling to understand how he could make himself right with God, and even in his brilliance, he could not find a way. Luther was so angry with God because he believed that God was demanding something of him that he himself could not do.

Then in the midst of reading Romans, Luther was stopped dead in his tracks by this phrase, "the righteousness of God through faith in Jesus Christ for all who believe" (Romans 3:22). The righteousness that comes from God is not our righteousness which gets us *to* God, but the righteousness of God that comes *from* God. And it is given to us as a gift through faith. Faith alone. Not faith plus works, not faith plus indulgences, not faith plus penance, not faith plus giving, not faith plus anything. It is simply faith alone in Christ.

Faith alone in Christ.

The righteousness of God is given freely to those who believe.

Now having faith is not believing *about* Jesus. The demons believe *about* Jesus. The demons have more faith than perhaps many who claim to be Christians. The Bible says, "Even the demons believe—and shudder" (James 2:19). They know who Jesus is. You can believe all the facts about Jesus. You can believe every Bible story, every Bible study, every sermon you ever heard that has been truth. You can believe all the facts and not have faith. Faith is not believing *about* Jesus. Faith is believing *on* Jesus.

Faith is believing *on* Jesus.

Hebrews 12:1-3 gives to us a great definition of faith:

> Therefore, since we are surrounded by so great a
> cloud of witnesses, let us also lay aside every
> weight, and sin which clings so closely, and let
> us run with endurance the race that is set before
> us, looking to Jesus, the founder and perfector of
> our faith, who for the joy that was set before
> him endured the cross, despising the shame,
> and is seated at the right hand of the throne of

God. Consider him who endured from sinners
such hostility against himself, so that you may
not grow weary or fainthearted.

Faith is looking to Jesus. That is what faith is. "Looking to Jesus, the founder and completer of our faith..." It's looking to Jesus, who is the one who died for you. We are to look away from ourselves and look to Christ. Look to him. That is faith.

Looking away from ourselves and looking to Christ.

A.W. Tozer said in Chapter 7 of his great book, *The Pursuit of God*, "Faith is the gaze of the soul on a saving God." Isn't that great? The gaze of the soul on God. Where are you looking for your salvation? If you're looking to your church, there's no salvation in any church. If you are looking to anything that *you* have done—a catechism, a confirmation, or to the merit of something you've accomplished in any way, there is no salvation there. Salvation comes by looking to Jesus. He endured the cross, the tree of death, to make it the tree of life for us. In looking to him, we receive the righteousness of God. It's a gift of grace. You don't have to earn it.

It's so beautifully simple. But it's the beautiful and humbling simplicity of the gospel that makes people stumble over it saying, "Tell me something to do. Give me a responsibility. What work do I need to accomplish? What great thing do I need to do for God?" There is nothing we can do. That is the reality. We are ruined. We are lost. We cannot save ourselves. But God has sent One who *can* do something—someone who can save us—the Lord Jesus Christ. And we become what he is. We become the righteousness of God when our faith is looking to him, and trusting in him.

Don't put your faith in a prayer that you prayed 30 or 40 years ago. Thank God that you prayed that prayer, but your prayer wasn't a perfect prayer. Thank God that you walked down an aisle, but you didn't walk down an aisle with perfect faith. Thank God that you got baptized, but you didn't get baptized with perfect faith. The reason you are saved is because someone perfect, perfectly substituted himself for your sins and satisfied the wrath of God. If you're looking to him, you are saved. Let me write this again because it's of the utmost importance. If you are looking toward Jesus, you are saved. Period. End of sentence.

Are you looking to Christ today? If you will look to Christ, let me tell you what's ahead for you. *You get to go back to the tree.* You get to go back to the garden because the way has been made open through Jesus Christ.

The Bible begins in the garden, with the Tree of Life, and God's image bearers enjoying him in his presence. Now let's look at Revelation 22:1-5 at where the Bible ends:

> Then the angel showed me the river of the water
> of life, bright as crystal, flowing from the throne
> of God and of the Lamb through the middle
> of the street of the city; also, on either side of
> the river, the tree of life with its twelve kinds of
> fruit, yielding its fruit each month. The leaves of
> the tree were for the healing of the nations. No
> longer will there be anything accursed, but the
> throne of God and of the Lamb will be in it,
> and his servants will worship him. They will see
> his face, and his name will be on their
> foreheads. And night will be no more. They will
> need no light of lamp or sun, for the Lord God
> will be their light, and they will reign forever
> and ever.

There is no Satan in this garden. Evil has been banished forever. There will be no more curse. There will only be the throne of God, and the Lamb will be sitting on the throne, and his servants will be worshiping him. Paradise lost, paradise redeemed. In Revelation 22:13-15, the Lord says:

I am the Alpha and the Omega, the first and the
last, the beginning and the end. Blessed are
those who wash their robes, so that they may
have the right to the *tree of life* and that they
may enter the city by the gates. Outside are the
dogs and sorcerers and the sexually immoral
and murderers and idolaters, and everyone who
loves and practices falsehood.
(Revelation 22:13-15)

Those who wash their robes have the right to "the Tree of Life." The Tree of the Knowledge of Good and Evil became the tree of evil. And the image bearers were expelled from the presence of God. But another image bearer came, a perfect image bearer, and lived the life that we should have lived. He allowed himself to be nailed to the tree of death, and on that tree, he conquered sin and Satan. Jesus took our sin and gave us his righteousness. And all those who look to him are granted the righteousness of God and inherit the privilege to enter the Kingdom, paradise once again, to eat of the Tree of Life, forever and ever, in an eternal homeland where there will never again be a curse.

The best way I know how, with the help of the Holy Spirit and the word of God, I have shared with you the gospel of Jesus Christ. This is the eternal everlasting gospel. Jesus gives salvation to all who look to him, so will you look to Christ? Look away from any confidence in prayers, in a church, catechism or confirmation, or Baptism. Look away from these, and look to Jesus—the author and completer of our faith. All who look to him and trust in him, are given the righteousness of God.

R.E.A.P. GUIDE

READ:

Romans 8:28-30
Galatians 5:22-23

EXAMINE:

1. What truth stood out to you from *In His Image,* Chapter 4?
2. How is the promise of Romans 8:28 so encouraging for followers of Jesus Christ? What should be included in "all things?"
3. Reading through Romans 8:29-30, who is the one performing all the action? Why do you think this is relevant?
4. In Romans 8:29, the main aim of God is for us "to be conformed to the image of his Son." Look at the words that describe you as a restored image bearer. How do those words bring you assurance?
5. Galatians 5:22-23 describes fruit that God the Holy Spirit produces in each believer. Where do you see

this fruit in the Lord Jesus' life? Where do you see this fruit being produced in your life?

APPLY:

- Do you really believe the promise that God is using "all things" in your life for the good of restoring you? Even the hard things? Make a list of the events going on in your life that God is using to restore you.
- Thank God for each of the items on your list, knowing he is in control of it all for your good and restoration.
- Think of another believer who is struggling right now. What tangible encouragement can you give him or her this week?

PRAY:

- When you talk to God, thank him for his unstoppable and secure plan to make you like his Son.
- Pray for boldness to live like a foreknown, predestined, called, justified and glorified image bearer.
- Commit to God those things that seem only to be for your hurt, trusting him to work out *all things* in your life for good.

PART IV: HIS IMAGE RENEWED

5

O, COME LET US ADORE HIM

So we do not lose heart. Though our outer self is
wasting away, our inner self is being renewed
day by day. For this light momentary affliction
is preparing for us an eternal weight of glory
beyond all comparison, as we look not to the
things that are seen but to the things that are
unseen. For the things that are seen are transient,
but the things that are unseen are eternal.
(2 Corinthians 4:16-18)

T his morning when I looked into the mirror, I saw this
Scripture fulfilled. The outer self is surely wasting
away! But, I also praised God that as I looked out
upon the beautiful world that God has given us, I took the
time to look into his word. And I experienced *this* Scripture

being fulfilled as well: "...our inner self is being renewed day by day." I rejoice in God my Savior because, yes, my body is growing older and weaker, but my spirit is forever young. I'm looking forward to the day when God will give me a forever young body to go with this forever young spirit. When those two get together, that will truly be heaven indeed.

The inner self is looking forward to the day when the total renewal of the outer-self coincides with the new self that we have in Jesus Christ. Existing forever in his image. That's what we long for. This book *In His Image* is about the process of what God is doing to make us and remake us in his image.

God's word outlines the process necessary to restore you and me into his image. Romans 8 speaks of God's eternal restoration project. God's plan is "eternal" because it has been planned from eternity. When Adam and Eve sinned, they did not take God by surprise. God the Father did not have to call the Holy Trinity into an emergency session and say, "What are we going to do?" God's plan of redeeming people is not plan B. It was God's plan A from eternity passed, that he would restore ruined image bearers. That is his plan.

GOD'S GOLDEN CHAIN OF SALVATION

And that plan A is eternal and it's personal. In Romans 8, apostle Paul outlines a golden chain of salvation. Written here are five golden gospel links that are tied together from eternity past to eternity future. This is God's plan of eternal salvation, and it is the plan for your personal salvation. It's awesome.

> And we know that for those who love God all things work together for good, for those who are called according to his purpose. For those whom he *foreknew* he also *predestined* to be conformed to the image of his Son, in order that he might be the firstborn among many brothers. And those whom he predestined he also *called*, and those whom he called he also *justified*, and those whom he justified he also *glorified*. (Romans 8:28-30)

Romans 8:29 says, "For those whom he foreknew..." That word "foreknew" means that God entered into a personal covenant relationship with his people before they were even created. In eternity past, he set his love on his people that their salvation would be accomplished. God *foreknew* them.

And out of that great love, God *predestined* them. "Predestined" means he marked them out to be his own. Those whom God set his love on, and had known in a covenant relationship before the world began, he marked them out to be his own.

God marked his people out to be his own.

In verse 30, Paul says that there came a time when those whom God foreknew and predestined, he also *called*. "Called" means there comes a moment in time when God *calls* ruined image bearers, sinners, to himself through the Holy Spirit. He brings them out of darkness and into the light of salvation. God *calls* them, and they come.

Paul continues in verse 30… "those whom he called he also justified." There is a moment when God—because of the merit of the Lord Jesus Christ and the worthiness of his atoning sacrifice on the cross—God declares *not guilty* those, who by faith, look to Jesus Christ as their Lord and Savior. Believers who look to Jesus are justified from all their sins. They are declared righteous, not based on their own righteousness, but by a righteousness from God himself.

Paul goes on to say that "those whom he justified he also glorified" (Romans 8:30). This hasn't happened yet, but it's amazing. We believers, have not yet been glorified, and yet it's so certain in God's mind that he uses the past tense. He has *already* glorified every single one of his children. He has already determined that they will be restored and that they will enjoy being glorified in his presence forever. Paradise regained.

These five steps of God's plan make up the golden chain of salvation and it reaches from eternity to eternity. For Christians, this is the chain that reunites our lives to God through Christ.

These five specific acts are all acts of God—he *foreknew*, he *predestined*, he *called*, he *justified*, and he *glorified*. But notice that this also involves a *process*. Between *justified* and *glorified*, there is a *lifetime*. Your lifetime. There is a period of time between when you were justified by faith and when you will be glorified in the resurrection. During this period of time, Christians experience a process whereby they are *sanctified*. In this process, we become more and more set apart to be God's own, and less and less to be *our* own.

Why was the word "sanctified" not mentioned in Scripture? Why didn't Paul say "those he justified, he glorified, he also sanctified?" The word "sanctified" is not there because Paul has already described what sanctification means in Romans 8:28-29. He says, "And we know that for those who love God all things work together for good, for those who are called according to his purpose. For those whom he foreknew he also predestined to be conformed to the image of his Son…"

There is a process going on in every Christian's life, and the process is a process of God conforming that believer, more and more, to the image of God's Son. God has a divine remodeling program going on! It's the remodeling of our lives, making us like the image of Christ. Now, when we think about God making us in his Son's image, we can't help but think back to the book of Genesis, and the story of Adam's creation. When God made man he announced, "'Let us make man in our image, after our likeness'" (Genesis 1:26).

We are told in a very powerful and poignant way, how God created man. He used the dirt of the earth. And with this, we have an image in our minds of Almighty God kneeling in the dirt, and taking dirt and forming it like a master craftsman into a human being. Adam was made in the image of God, but that image was soon terribly marred by sin. And all of us now, as descendants of our human ancestors Adam and Eve, are corrupted. Our image bearing of God is corrupted by our own sin nature and our own personal sin.

But God's plan is a plan of reforming that corrupted image. With the power of his Spirit, God proclaims, *"I'm going to remodel my image bearers but this time I'm going to use a perfect model."* And the model that he uses to form us is the model of his Son, the Lord of Glory. Through our salvation in Christ a process begins by God's Spirit to remodel us as image bearers. We are made more and more like the perfect image bearer himself—the Son of God, Jesus Christ.

That's the gospel, and the gospel is an *action*. It is a continuing process of God working in our lives. He's remodeling us to form us to the image of his Son. That's God's promise and that's God's *process*. How does God do this? What are the means God uses to remodel us in his image? And how can I as a weak and sinful person, facilitate what God is doing? We are not neutral in this. We are *active responders* in this process of sanctification.

So how does God actually remodel us? There are three primary and personal responses by which we enter into and facilitate this work of God in our lives. The first response by which we participate with God in this process, is through *adoration*.

ADORATION

It is through our adoration of God, our worship, that we are renewed as God's image bearers. The renewal process happens while we are with him. It is in the presence of God that he does his work of changing us most effectively and most powerfully. Worship is always to be connected in our minds with the concept of being *in the presence of God*.

The Greek word most often used for worship in the New Testament is the word *proskuneo*. *Pros* means "toward." *Kuneo* means "to kiss." Worship then means to "kiss toward." It is an image from the ancient middle east, of someone coming into the presence of a ruler, a king, or a high official. That person would bow forward and often kiss the ground on which the king or ruler was standing. Or, at other times, one would go to his knees, lean forward, and kiss the ring or the signet that was on the ruler or the king's finger. He would "kiss toward" the official.

What does that tell us about worship? Worship combines two great qualities: *Reverence* and *love*. Worship is the act of expressing reverential love toward God. It contains fear, reverence, devotion, and adoration. It is an expression of reverential love. And it is so powerful because it is in worship, as we are expressing reverential love to our creator, that we are being renewed and changed.

2 Corinthians is the most personal, autobiographical letter apostle Paul ever wrote. In it, he expresses the things of his heart—his life, his journey, his testimony—because he's been so discredited by his enemies in Corinth. People were asking, "Where are Paul's letters? If he is such a great leader, where are the testimonies?" In Chapter 3 Paul says, *"Do I really need letters of introduction? Listen to me. You are my letters of introduction. If somebody wants to know the truth of my ministry, if somebody wants to know the truth that I have been faithful to God, if somebody wants to*

know the reality of the gospel, you are my letters of accreditation. Your lives are my letters. You are living epistles."

> And you show that you are a letter from Christ
> delivered by us, written not with ink but with
> the Spirit of the living God, not on tablets of
> stone but on tablets of human hearts.
> (2 Corinthians 3:3)

Paul then describes the giving of the Old Covenant. Moses went up the mountain and was given the law on the tablets of stone. When he came down, his face was shining so brightly with the glory of God that nobody could look at him. They asked Moses to put a veil over his face but over a period of time, the glory of the Lord slowly faded so Moses could eventually remove the veil.

Paul explains that the Old Covenant, the law, has faded away. It possessed a glory, the glory of Mount Sinai, but that glory is fading away because there is a new glory that has come. That new glory is the glory of the *New Covenant* of the Spirit. This is not the Old Covenant of the Law, made up of words on stone, but the New Covenant of the Spirit, which is the work of the word of God inscribed in someone's heart. This covenant never fades away, but instead shines and shines with greater and greater glory.

Then Paul makes this amazing analogy. He says that when people are looking to the Law to save them, it's like having a veil of disbelief over their face. It's as if a veil is covering their eyes and they cannot see the gospel. Then Paul says something so beautiful:

> But when one turns to the Lord [when they
> repent and have faith in Jesus], the veil is
> removed. [The inability to see the glory of God
> in Christ, is removed.] Now the Lord is the
> Spirit, [the Holy Spirit does this], and where the
> Spirit of the Lord is, there is freedom.
> (2 Corinthians 3:16-17)

Freedom! Not the old bondage to the Law, but now full liberty in Christ. Let's focus on this amazing verse:

> And we all, with unveiled face, beholding the
> glory of the Lord, are being transformed into the
> same image from one degree of glory to
> another. For this comes from the Lord who is
> the Spirit." (2 Corinthians 3:18)

Notice that there is an *action*, and then there's a *result*. There's an action that brings a result. What is the action? The action in verse 18 is "beholding the glory of the Lord…" The action is "looking to the glory of the Lord."

That's the action—looking to the Lord. And here is the result—we are "being transformed into the same image."

Paul reveals that as people turn to the Lord and begin to worship Jesus, they are being transformed into the same image of the Lord. They are being changed. They are becoming more and more like Jesus. From glory to glory they are being changed by the Spirit of God. Paul says, "They are being transformed." The word transformed means *metamorphosis*. People who are focusing on the Lord are going through a metamorphosis. A metamorphosis means a significant change from the inside out. It means to be changed from within so that the new person is shining out of the old person.

Do you remember the story of Jesus on the mountain of transfiguration? The Bible says he was *transfigured* in the presence of his three disciples. This word "transfigured" is the same word for metamorphosis. Jesus went through a metamorphosis before their very eyes. The inner Jesus, the eternal Son of God, shined through the body of Jesus of Nazareth. So, the three disciples: Simon Peter, James, and John saw the Son of God, not in the physical body that contained him, but in the reality of who he really is.

Paul says the same thing happens to us. As we worship the Lord, as we begin to shift our focus from ourselves and the world to the Lord, a metamorphosis takes place so that more and more of the new you shines through the old you. Incredible, isn't it?! It's an *ongoing* and an *on growing* change from one degree of glory to another. And where does this change take place? It takes place in the presence of God. In worship. The metamorphosis takes place when we are *"Beholding the glory of the Lord."*

Now how do you participate in or facilitate this process? How do you behold the glory of the Lord? You do it in a very simple but costly way. If you want your life to be changed, if you want to grow and be more like Jesus, you must *spend time with him.*

You will never experience renewal on the run.

Worship is being in the Lord's presence. It's so simple, but it's so costly because it costs you what is most precious to you. It costs you time. Personal worship takes time. You will never experience renewal on the run. And you will never become holy in a hurry. If you truly want to be an image bearer of God, if you want to be more and more like Jesus, you've got to find the time to sit at his feet. You must schedule time to be with him, open his word, open your heart, open your ears to listen, and open your mouth to talk with him. All this takes time.

When you set aside time to be in the presence of the Lord, when you open up his word and allow him to speak, and open your ears to hear, and open your heart to listen to what God is saying, *it's happening.*

> And we all, with unveiled face, beholding the
> glory of the Lord, are being transformed into the
> same image from one degree of glory to
> another. For this comes from the Lord who is
> the Spirit. (2 Corinthians 3:18)

When you are in his presence, you are being renewed into God's image.

The church that I am blessed to pastor has a wonderful ministry called Renew. Renew is a recovery ministry for those who have experienced, or are experiencing, the bondage of substance abuse. We didn't call it, "Recovery," because *recovering* is not the goal. The goal of the Lord is not for people just to *recover*. The goal of the Lord is for people to be *renewed*. To "recover" means you're better but you're still the same. You have recovered from an illness. You're better but you're the same. To be "renewed" though, means that you have been transformed. You're better, but you're not the same person you use to be. A change has occurred in your very identity. You have been renewed, and that's what the Lord is revealing in 2 Corinthians 3:18. "And we all, with unveiled face, beholding the glory of the Lord, are being transformed into the same image from one degree of glory to another. For this comes from the Lord who is the Spirit."

The renewal process takes time. You can't rush it. You can't microwave this miracle. We're so used to microwaves, aren't we? Three minutes seems like a lifetime as we stand there and wait. We have grown to expect the same instant gratification in our spiritual life as well.

"I go to church pretty often. That's got to count for something."

"I don't have time to actually read the Bible because I'm just too busy. So, when I'm in the car, I put in a CD."

"I talk to the Lord when I'm at the gym."

"I get it. Really, I do. But I have important responsibilities and I'm a very busy person. I don't have time to sit there and think about God."

The renewal process is so simple, but it's going to cost you your most precious commodity—time. You are given 168 golden hours every week. If you want renewal, you are going to have to find times during those 168 hours to be in the presence of the Lord.

There are great books that people can recommend to you, but there's no book like *The* Book, the Bible. There are wonderful resources that people can recommend to help you, but there's no resource like the resource of the Holy Spirit. There are wonderful tools that people could share with you, but nothing is as powerful as spending time with Jesus. He's the answer. Talk to him like he's there, because, you know what? He is there! And he desires a relationship with you.

Talk to Jesus like he's there because he is.

Open his word. Open the Bible. You might ask, "Where do I start?" I would recommend the Gospels (Matthew, Mark, Luke, and John) but the most important thing is to just start! Say out loud, "Lord, you are the author of this book. You are the God who renews people into your image. I'm seeking you. I just want to be here with you. I'm listening. Speak to me. I'm worshiping you." You do that and guess what? It starts happening. The transformation. Not immediately. It's not microwaved. But the process is real. And when you start, it starts.

If you want to bear the image of Christ, you must *be* with him. Jesus' first call to every disciple is, "Follow me. Come, be with me." Being a Christian is not about getting to heaven when you die. That's the outcome, yes. But being a Christian means that you follow Jesus, day by day and that you are *with him.*

"So we do not lose heart. Though our outer self is wasting away, our inner self is being renewed day by day" (2 Corinthians 4:16). Spend time with Jesus and this is the promised outcome—a true inner metamorphosis.

R.E.A.P. GUIDE

READ:

Romans 8:26-30
1 Cor. 15:49
2 Cor. 3:18
Col. 3:10
1 John 3:2

EXAMINE:

1. What did God teach you through *In His Image,* Chapter 5?
2. From the passages listed in the "Read" section above, list three of God's promises presented and refer to them during the week.
3. What is the source of assurance given in these passages that provide the confidence these promises will become a reality?
4. Romans 8:28 is one of the most quoted passages of Scripture by believers. How does reading this verse within the context of the entire passage, impact your

thoughts concerning its meaning?

APPLY:

- There are over 3000 promises made by God in the Bible! God will bring to fruition everything he has said that he will do. Chapter 5 of *In His Image* is anchored in the promise God has given to renew his image in his people. From the moment you became a disciple of Jesus Christ, the indwelling presence of the Holy Spirit initiated a life-long process of renewing the damaging effect of sin in you. Describe one or two ways in which the Holy Spirit has brought renewal into your life?
- One of the benefits gained from understanding God's promises is that his people may live with confidence and assurance. The truths that you have gained from this chapter, and studying the passages listed, should result in trusting God to faithfully do all that he has promised, even when you are confronted with uncertainty and doubt (Hebrews 11:1). In what areas of your life can you be intentionally trusting God more?

PRAY:

- Often, doubt and fear will become more intense when you embrace the truth of God's promises found in Scripture. You must trust God, even during these moments of insecurity. Ask him for comfort and guidance.
- When praying this week, offer God praise and adoration for the surety of his word and all the promises he has made. Ask him for a day-by-day renewal of the determination required to walk in a manner worthy of the calling he has placed on your life. Give thanks to him for renewing you into the image of Christ, even in those moments when you feel you are falling short of his expectations.

6

EMBRACING HIS PURPOSE

Several years ago, I was invited to join the board of a small mission that a friend of mine was leading. He tempted me by telling me that the annual board meeting was in Orlando, Florida…in February! I prayed about that for about fifteen seconds then said, "Yes!"

The first board meeting that I attended was in a large conference room in the hotel, and just so happened to take place on my birthday. I knew no one else on the board, so you can imagine my surprise when I entered the room and the entire place was decked out in birthday celebration paraphernalia. There were floating balloons, a beautiful cake and punch. I'm thinking, "How did they know? This is amazing. These are the nicest people I've ever met."

I stood there drinking some of my own punch saying hello to a few people when the meeting finally began. The leader said, "Okay, let's sing happy birthday to our honored guest." All the people in the room started singing happy birthday. I was standing there smiling and taking it all in until they came to the end of the song. "Happy birthday, dear *Bob*. Happy birthday to you."

Bob?! Yes, there was an elderly gentleman in attendance, also a member of the board, and all who had gathered were celebrating *his* birthday. The Lord certainly has a way of humbling you sometimes! I can almost see him elbowing Gabriel and saying, "Hey, Gabe. Watch this."

I walked over to this man named Bob and I said, "You're not going to believe this, Bob, but this is my birthday too."

He said, "This is *your* birthday?"

I said, "Yes, today is my birthday."

"Well, I'm glad to share my birthday party with you. Happy birthday."

"Thank you so much." I then asked Bob, "Where are you from?"

He said, "I was born in a place you've never heard of in your life. I was born in Henry County, Indiana."

"Where?" I asked.

"Henry County, Indiana."

I replied, "*I* was born in Henry County, Indiana!"

He said, "No, you weren't!"

I said, "I was! I was born in Henry County, Indiana. February 19th." I then asked Bob, "Where specifically were you born in Henry County, Indiana?"

Bob replied, "Do you remember the Greensboro Pike?"

"Greensboro Pike? Of course! There was a country store there where my father use to take me and my brothers to get some candy and soda."

He said, "Well, you know that farmhouse right across from the Greensboro Pike?"

"Yes."

"I was born in that farmhouse." (About this time I was expecting *The Twilight Zone* theme music to start!)

While serving on that board, I had a chance to get to know Bob. I learned that he and his father had invented the Reese Trailer Hitch. Bob's business prospered and he became quite wealthy. He was a devout follower of the Lord and was also rich in his generosity. He was determined that he and his wife would give away most of their resources to the work of the Lord.

Now, what were the odds of us two meeting? Can you imagine? On our birthdays, to be in Florida, in the same room, sharing the same birthday, and both of us having been born in the same county. That was amazing. We shared the same birth day and the same birth place, but as Christians, Bob and I also shared something else—we shared the same birth *purpose*. God gave both of us eternal life for the same purpose. And it's the same purpose he gave you for your birth, if you're a Christian.

The purpose of our birth as Christians has been stated clearly in Romans 8:29: "For those whom he foreknew he also predestined to be conformed to the image of his Son, in order that he might be the firstborn among many brothers." The Lord Jesus brought us to life that we might be conformed to his image. God, who has saved us, has saved us that we might be conformed to the image of his Son. Every Christian may not share the same birthday *physically*, or *spiritually*, but every Christian shares the same *birth purpose*.

We were born again, not just to get us into heaven when we die, but to be made image bearers of God. We are to be made into the likeness of Jesus, and renewed in his image. This is what this book, *In His Image,* is all about. In Chapter 5 we asked the question, "How does the Lord make us like Jesus? How does he start the process that he is going to complete one day? What is that process?" And also very important, "How do we facilitate that process while God is working in our hearts to make us more into the image of his Son?"

There are three words that guide us in the process of becoming more like Jesus. We've discussed the first word—*adoration.* We are transformed through our worship. It is in his presence that we are renewed as his image bearers, not only on Sunday morning, but during personal, private worship as well. God's intention through the local church is to use public time of worship to make us more like Jesus Christ. As we allow that process to be facilitated in our lives, we are changed. Paul describes the process in 2 Corinthians 3:16. "But when one turns to the Lord, the veil is removed." The veil is the blindness that keeps us from seeing the glory of God in the face of Jesus Christ. When one believes, repents, and turns to the Lord, the veil is removed.

> Now the Lord is the Spirit, and where the Spirit
> of the Lord is, there is freedom. And we all,
> with unveiled face, beholding the glory of the
> Lord [ADORATION/WORSHIP], are being
> transformed into the same image from one
> degree of glory to another. For this comes from
> the Lord who is the Spirit.
> (2 Corinthians 3:17-18)

How do we facilitate this miracle of the Spirit? There is an action and the result. As we are worshiping the Lord, as we are in his presence, as we are focusing our attention on the glory of God in Christ, we are being transformed into the same image. This is God's plan—for us to be conformed to the image of his Son. This miraculous process takes place as we are in the presence of the Lord, worshiping him, through *adoration*.

COOPERATION

We also participate in God's process through *cooperation*, or our will. We are being formed in the image of Christ through our a*doration* and by our will in *cooperation*. We cooperate with God. Only God can redeem a life. We can't redeem ourselves. Only God can restore and renew a life, but it's important to understand that we are not neutral in this process. You will never read anywhere in the Bible that you just sit around with your arms crossed and say, "Go ahead, God. Do it." We are called upon by God to respond to him, to his love, and to his Spirit. We are certainly not called to be neutral. By God's grace, and his enablement, we cooperate with him as he works in our lives.

**We must cooperate with God
as he works in our lives.**

Paul says something about this process in Philippians 2:12-13. He says "work out" your salvation. But notice, he didn't say "work *for*..." He said, "Work *out*..."

> Therefore, my beloved, as you have
> always obeyed, so now, not only as in my
> presence but much more in my absence, *work
> out* your own salvation with fear and trembling,

for it is God who works in you, both to will and
to work for his good pleasure.

We are to *work out* our salvation in cooperation with God,
knowing that God is working within us. And we must
cooperate. What does it look like when a person begins to
cooperate with God in his or her life? Romans 12:1
describes two ways in which we cooperate with God as he
is working within us to renew our lives. The first way we
cooperate is by *relinquishing*. Letting go and letting God.
The following verse may be quite familiar, but see if you
can enjoy it again for the very first time:

I appeal to you therefore, brothers, by the
mercies of God, to present your bodies as a
living sacrifice, holy and acceptable to God,
which is your spiritual worship. (Romans 12:1)

We cooperate with the Lord by *relinquishing* our control.

Maybe you've heard the story of the man who was
hiking along a trail that took him around the very edge of a
mountain. Suddenly, he tripped and fell off the edge. There
was a tree growing out of the side of that mountain, and
miraculously as the man fell, he caught one of those limbs
as he was falling down. So, imagine, here he was hanging
between heaven and earth, with only his grip on that limb
to keep him from certain death.

He began to cry out for help, and then he heard a voice that seemed to come right out from the clouds. The voice said, "Do you believe that I put that tree there for you?"

"Yes! Yes! Yes! I believe!"

The voice said, "Do you believe that I am able to send the wind and blow you right back up on that cliff?"

"Yes, yes. I believe."

And then the voice said, "All right. Now, *let go.*"

The man hung there for a moment and then he replied, "Is there anybody else up there I could talk to?"

How we hate to let go. This is so true it needs repeating. How we hate to let go!!!

We say, "Lord, I want to be different."

The Lord says, "Let me help you out."

We say, "Lord, I want you to change me."

The Lord says, "Let me show you my plan."

We say, "Lord, use me!"

And the Lord says, "Now, let me tell you what I'm thinking."

And we don't listen.

How we hate to relinquish control. Yet, you can't cooperate and control at the same time. I'm sure you've seen the signs that read, "God is my co-pilot." But let me say this, if God is your co-pilot, you're in the wrong seat! Someone once said, perhaps more appropriately, "God is not my co-pilot. God is my *pilot* and I'm on the stretcher in the back of the plane!"

You cannot cooperate and control at the same time. You've got to let go. This is Paul's appeal in Romans 12:1. "I appeal to you therefore, brothers…" Every word in this verse is just filled with significance. The word "appeal" or "urge" is as if someone comes alongside you, puts their arm around you, and pleads with you.

> I appeal to you therefore, brothers, by the
> mercies of God, to present your bodies as a
> living sacrifice, holy and acceptable to God,
> which is your spiritual worship. (Romans 12:1)

"I'm begging you brothers," is the idea here. "And I'm pleading with you on the basis of the mercies of God in your life. The mercies of your salvation. The mercies of your adoption into the family of God. The mercies of the promise of your glorification." If you wanted to give a title to the first half of the book of Romans, chapters 1 to 11, it could be *The Mercies of God*. Those chapters are about how God takes a dead, doomed sinner, and transforms him into one who inherits glory. Paul says "I'm begging you, based on the mercies of God, to present your bodies…" The word "present" here means a definite act. It means something that is deliberately done at a point in time. I appeal to you by the mercies of God that you decide to present your body to God as a living sacrifice. Your body, is in fact, *his* body.

The common denominator of every animal sacrifice in the Old Testament was that they all died. They were all slain, just as Christ would be slain. But now we do not have to offer sacrifices to God as a part of our salvation because Christ has offered himself to God once and for all. Christ is the perfect sacrifice. Now we must make a decision to present *our body* as a *living* sacrifice. A living surrender. Not dead. Fully alive, but fully surrendered. Holy. Set apart for God. When my body and my life are set apart for God, it is acceptable, which means it is well-pleasing to him. The sacrifice pleasing to God is when you present your body to be set apart to him.

Paul says that this is our *spiritual* worship. The word "spiritual" here is from the Greek word *logikan*. We get our word *logical* from this word. It is your logical act of worship. When you think about the mercies of God in your life, isn't presenting yourself to Jesus the only logical thing to do? It is your spiritual, your logical, your rational, worship service to him and for him.

When you leave church following a worship service, the Lord wants the worship service to continue. As you are living for him, your life becomes a living worship. I heard a preacher say many years ago, at the end of his worship services, "Our meeting is over. Now the service begins."

Paul is talking about relinquishing. Are you going to let go? What are you clutching in your life? What are you trying to control? Will you relinquish your future to the

Lord? Will you relinquish your past? How does the Lord make us like Jesus? He does it when we have the attitude of Jesus who said, "I have come to do my Father's will. I've come to cooperate with my Father." This is how transformation begins.

As Christians, we cooperate in this process of restoration by *relinquishing*, but we also cooperate by *resisting*. That sounds like a contradiction in terms, doesn't it? "We are to cooperate by resisting." But that's exactly what Paul is doing here. He's using this contradiction of terms to grip us. He's talking about relinquishing control and then, after having relinquished control to God, Paul says, "Now I want you to resist."

> Do not be conformed to this world, but be
> transformed by the renewal of your mind, that
> by testing you may discern what is the will of
> God, what is good and acceptable and perfect.
> (Romans 12:2)

Here again, every word is so incredibly purposeful and important. As you are now relinquishing the control of your life to God, Paul says, "I want you to resist." Do not be conformed to this world. It is literally this, "Stop being conformed to this world. Stop letting the world press you into its mold." Paul is not referring to the *world* here as the planet. He's talking about the spirit of the world. The values of the world. The culture. "Stop letting the world press you into its mold." He's saying, "Be different. Break the mold. Be free."

Be different. Break the mold. Be free.

We hear so much about this today. It's almost laughable if it were not so sad that the people who think they are being *different*, the people who think they are being *real*, the people who think they are being an *individual* are just letting themselves be pressed into the world's mold. They are not different at all. They are saying, "Let's find out what's in style and do that." That's what being different is like for those who are not yet able to relinquish their lives as a living sacrifice to the Lord. "Let's figure out what the world thinks these days, and do that." That's not being different. That's being the same. It's humbling to be different. After all, who wants to be part of the "odd for God" squad? The question is, do you want to be free or accepted? Paul says, "I want you to be free."

Thomas Jefferson, the principal author of the Declaration of Independence said this, "I have sworn upon the altar of God eternal hostility against every form of tyranny over the mind of man." Where does the Declaration of Independence begin? It begins in the mind. Likewise, the Lord wants our minds to be set free. It's God's plan to renew us as image bearers by renewing our mind. How does

God change us? The change has to happen in our minds. "Do not be conformed to this world, but be transformed by the renewal of your mind" (Romans 12:2). God transforms us by transforming our minds.

You can see Paul's play on words even in the English translation. *"Don't be conformed but be transformed..."* Don't be conformed to the world's mold where you are being pressed into a position where what you *really are* is not what you appear to be on the outside. The world is pressing you into a mold that is not really you. Don't be conformed; be transformed. Transformed means to be *externally* who you really are *internally*.

Transformed means to be *externally* who you really are *internally*.

The word for transformed is *metamorphosis*. As we are beholding the glory of the Lord we are being transformed; we are going through a metamorphosis. The real you who is in Christ, is becoming stronger and more dominant. The new nature you have is breaking through this mold of the external, so that the real you is showing. You are being transformed. That is what Paul is talking about. "Don't let the world press you into its mold, but instead, break the mold by having your mind renewed which lets the real you that is in Christ, come out."

Jesus had something to say about the renewal of people's minds. He prayed passionately for all believers.

Jesus prayed for your mind to be renewed.

In his prayer in the garden of Gethsemane, Jesus said, "I do not ask for these only, but also for those who will believe in me through their word..." (John 17:20). He was praying for *those* as well—for you and for me. And here's what Jesus prayed, "Sanctify them in the truth; your word is truth (John 17:17)." Sanctify them. Change them. Set them apart. The idea here is to renew. "Father, renew them through your truth; your word is truth." Jesus did not say, "Your word is true," though every word of God is true. He said, "Your word is *truth*."

Truth is not relative. Truth is objective. Truth is fixed. Jesus said that truth does not change from culture to culture, or age to age. It does not change from poll to poll. "God's word is truth." The Scriptures are the objective standard of truth. How does the Lord change us? He changes us with the truth.

Jesus said in John 8:32, "You will know the truth, and the *truth shall set you free*." Now recall Paul's words. "But when one turns to the Lord, the veil is removed. Now the Lord is the Spirit, and where the Spirit of the Lord is, there is freedom" (2 Corinthians 3:16-17). Freedom comes from

God, and he sets us free when our minds are being renewed by truth. It is the truth that sets us free.

It is the truth that sets us free.

The power of the living God is the word of God that you are able to hear in church and the word of God that you are able to read throughout the week. Its purpose is to renew your mind. "You will know the truth, and the truth will set you free." "Father, I pray for my people," Jesus said. "Sanctify them in the truth [set them apart]; your word is truth." (John 17:17).

One of the most hideous of all the Nazi concentration camps was one named Auschwitz. Over one million Jewish men and women, boys and girls, were gassed to death at Auschwitz. Their bodies were incinerated. A sign hung above the gate to what they were told would be their place of work. The sign contained these words, "Work makes you free." What a monstrous lie! The Nazis had no intention for them to be free. The Nazis intention was to work the Jews to death, and just before that, to gas them to death—to incinerate them. "Work makes you free." It's a terrible lie.

Satan is the master of monstrous lies, except he presents the lies to us a little differently. For some people he whispers, *I know what you want out of life and hard work will get it for you. Hard work will make you free.* There are Christians by the thousands who believe that lie and yet every day they live by that principle. They say to themselves, "I live to work because I believe that work will set me free."

Others believe this lie of Satan's. *"Money makes you free. If you have enough money, you can do what you want, when you want, where you want, and how you want. Money makes you free. So, do whatever you can to make lots of money. It doesn't matter how, because the end result will be worth it."* Money doesn't set you free. It's a lie. "For what does it profit a man to gain the whole world and forfeit his soul" (Mark 8:36).

"Power makes you free!" *"Success makes you free!"* *"Popularity makes you free!"* Those are all lies. A Christian may work hard. He or she may love people. He or she may strive for excellence. But he or she does that *not* because work makes them free, or money makes them free, or popularity makes them free. He or she does it because the *truth* is making them free, and that truth is in Jesus. And "…if the Son sets you free, you will be free indeed" (John 8:36).

R.E.A.P. GUIDE

READ:

    Philippians 2:12-13
    1 Thessalonians 5:23
    Hebrews 13:20-21
    Romans 6:13, 8:13, 12:1
    Hebrews 12:14
    1 Thessalonians 4:3
    2 Corinthians 7:1
    2 Peter 1:5

EXAMINE:

1. What truth stood out to you from *In His Image,* Chapter 6?
2. Philippians 2:12-13 shares the truth that God has a part in your sanctification and you also have a part. What are those parts?
3. 1 Thessalonians 5:23 and Hebrews 13:20-21 speak of God's role in your sanctification. What can you count on God to do in your life according to these

verses?

4. Romans 6:13, 8:13 and 12:1 are commands related to the believer's "passive" role in sanctification. "Passive" refers to our dependence on God. How do these verses command you in that "passive" responsibility?

5. Hebrews 12:14, 1 Thessalonians 4:3, 2 Corinthians 7:1, and 2 Peter 1:5 are commands related to the believer's "active" role in sanctification. What does God command us to actively pursue so we will grow into Christ's image?

APPLY:

- Most of us have heard the expression, "Let go and let God" in connection with our spiritual growth. In light of what you have read in the Bible, would you consider this good counsel for someone? Why or why not?

- What happens to us if we neglect the "passive" role of trusting God to sanctify us?

- What happens to us if we neglect the "active" role of obeying God and "working out our own salvation" (Philippians 2:12)?

- As you examine your life, are you in any way out of balance between the "passive" work and the "active" work of sanctification? If so, where are you more focused and why? What might help you grow in both areas?

PRAY:

- As you talk to God in prayer, thank him for being at work in you to make you like Christ! Meditate on God's character and trustworthiness.
- Talk to God about areas where you still desire to grow to be more like Christ. Yield your life to him in prayer.
- Ask him to continue changing your desires and actions as you purpose to obey him.

7

THE GREAT EXPECTATION

T hroughout this book we've been on a journey discovering what it means for us to be the image bearers of God. It's an amazing truth, when we sit back and think about it, that every human being is created in his image. We're thankful for the incredible redemption the Lord has given us as he redeems us as his image bearers. It's all part of his great salvation plan.

Let's look again at one of the most beloved passages of Scripture, as we consider what it shares regarding what God is doing in our lives:

> And we know that for those who love God all
> things work together for good, for those who are
> called according to his purpose. For those whom
> he foreknew he also predestined to be
> conformed to the image of his Son, in order that

he might be the firstborn among many brothers.
And those whom he predestined he also called,
and those whom he called he also justified, and
those whom he justified he also glorified.
(Romans 8:28-30)

The focus in verse 29 is on God's purpose which is to conform us to the image of his Son. God's purpose is not just to get us to heaven to be with him. His purpose is to truly make us what we were created to be—the image bearers of God. To be like his Son who is the perfect image bearer of Almighty God.

God's divine activities are things that God alone can do. God *foreknew* us, that is he knew us in a love relationship before the creation of the heavens and the earth. And then the Bible says he *predestined* us, which means he marked us out as his own. Then God says that those he predestined, he *called*, and that is the call that draws people to Jesus Christ. This does not just involve the hearing of the word, but the hearing of the *truth* which is empowered by the Spirit. This is what draws a person in faith to Jesus Christ. And those that he called, he *justified*. He declared them righteous due to the perfect atonement of Jesus Christ, who on the cross, became our sin and gave us his righteousness. Our sin is placed to Christ's account and his righteousness is placed to our account. We're not made spiritually neutral. We're made righteous with the righteousness that is not our own, but the righteousness of Christ. What a Savior! And those that he justified, he also *glorified*. God does all those actions.

But we have one area where we do have personal participation. We cannot *foreknow* ourselves. We cannot *predestine* ourselves. We cannot *call* ourselves. We cannot *justify* ourselves. We certainly cannot *glorify* ourselves. But we are participants in God's purpose as he conforms us to the image of his Son. We are not neutral chess pieces on a global divine chess board. We are participants in the work of God on this Earth, and we are participants in the work of God in our own hearts. Now, how do we facilitate God's process? How do we participate in what he is doing in us?

ADORATION

As we have discussed, there are three primary ways in which we can respond to what God is doing. For the benefit of review, the first was through *adoration*. We are being made more and more into the image of his Son when we are truly worshiping him.

I have difficulty understanding why people come to church with a downcast, depressed attitude. When we come to worship, we know that we are not going to leave the same as when we entered. How exciting! We will be changed, and that's not just when we gather in worship but when we are consistently spending time with the Lord. We are becoming like Moses who, after being in the presence of the Lord, came down from the mountain with his face shining. And we are told that he didn't even know his face was shining. We may not be aware of the transformation, but people around us are observing it and it's all to the glory of Christ.

COOPERATION

The second way we can respond to what God is doing in us is through our *cooperation*. We cooperate by *relinquishing* control and *resisting* the pressure to conform. By God's grace, we resist the pressure of the world to conform, and then we cooperate by agreeing with God as he does the work of renewing our lives. We must simply allow this incredible change to take place. The truth of the matter is, our biggest problem lies between our own two ears. It's the mind. We talk about the heart but the heart really is between our ears.

> Do not be conformed to this world, but be
> transformed by the renewal of your mind, that
> by testing you may discern what is the will of
> God, what is good and acceptable and perfect.
> (Romans 12:2).

It is our mind that needs renewal. It needs to be washed. Some people say they don't believe in brain washing. I don't know about you but my brain needs to be washed. And regularly.

EXPECTATION

The third word describing our involvement in this transformational process is the idea of living in *expectation*. We are to wait before the Lord. This is not inactivity. This is a very active waiting. And *as* we are waiting for the Lord, we are being changed. He is changing us internally as we are worshiping and studying his word. But there is another change that is going to happen, even more than changing us internally. God intends to change us *externally* and *eternally*. We are going to be changed on the outside as well. That's the reality of our resurrection hope. We are not everything we are going to be because there is a resurrection hope, and as we focus on the reality of that hope, we are being changed.

Sometimes we are told that there is *reality* and then there is *hope*. But when you're a Christian, your reality *is* your hope, because for us hope is not a contradiction; it is not wishful thinking. Hope does not mean *wanting* something to happen. Hope is steadfast assurance about what is *going* to happen because God has said it's going to happen. And the reality of our hope is found in the resurrection. The hope of what's going to happen when the Lord Jesus Christ gives us that final change, that hope is what is changing us right now.

Some of you have been Christians for years. Do you relate to the lyrics by Robert Robinson in the hymn *Come Thou Font of Every Blessing*? "Prone to wander, Lord, I feel it. Prone to leave the God I love." Have you ever felt that way? Certainly, we all realize how much change yet needs to take place in our lives. So, what is it we have to look forward to? In the resurrection, we are to expect an incredible change within our bodies. "So is it with the resurrection of the dead. What is sown is perishable; what is raised is imperishable" (1 Corinthians 15:42). That's talking about us—our body. It is sown in dishonor. It is raised in glory. It is sown in weakness. It is raised in power. It is sown a natural body, but it is raised a spiritual body. We will be raised with a spiritual body in the resurrection— a body fit for the spiritual world to which we are going. Our bodies are going to be changed and aren't we grateful to God for that?!

All of us are growing older, (some of us more than others), and we see the *sag, bag, and drag* that's going on. I am more than ready for the new edition. In the resurrection, our bodies will be incredibly changed, and our *image* is going to be changed as well. We are going to experience an extreme image makeover.

"Thus it is written, 'The first man Adam became a living being' [God formed him]; the last Adam became a life-giving spirit" (1 Corinthians 15:45). That doesn't mean that Jesus came as a spirit or that he rose again as a spirit. What this means is when he rose again, his spirit was life-giving. The first Adam became a living being. The last Adam became a life-giving spirit. But it's not the *spiritual* that is first; it's the *natural* that is first. The natural body first, then the spiritual body. The first man was from the earth and was a man of dust. The second man, Jesus, came from heaven.

"As was the man of dust, so also are those who are of the dust, and as is the man of heaven, so also are those who are of heaven" (1 Corinthians 15:48). Yes, we are of dust and the earth but we possess what Jesus has given us. As a life-giving spirit, Jesus has given us the new birth. We are God's children. We are his heavenly people on Earth in these earthly bodies. Now, here is the promise. "Just as we have borne the image of the man of dust, we shall also bear the image of the man of heaven" (1 Corinthians 15:49). We will perfectly bear his image. It's going to be an incredible change of our bodies and our very image.

When this change finally happens, it will not be a lingering process. The far Eastern religions talk about cycles of reincarnation, gradually moving from a lower to a higher form. That is not how the change is going to happen. We are going to be immediately altered.

So, how immediate is "immediately?"

> Behold! I tell you a mystery. [This is something
> that has never been revealed before.] We shall
> not all sleep, but we shall all be changed, in a
> moment, in the twinkling of an eye, [in an atom
> of time], at the last trumpet.
> (1 Corinthians 15:51-52)

Twinkling here means the amount of time it takes for light to reflect off of your eye. That quickly. In an *atom* of time. In a moment, like the reflecting of light off your eye, the last trumpet will sound. "For the trumpet will sound, and the dead will be raised imperishable, and we shall be changed" (1 Corinthians 15:52). We shall be changed into our spiritual, heavenly body. This will be the body we will have for the world to come. It will be given to us in an atom of time. It will happen in a twinkling of an eye. Those dead and those who are alive will be changed.

It's going to happen in a moment, but it's not going to last for just a moment because notice—we are going to be *immediately* changed but we are also going to be *immortally* changed. Immediate but immortal. Alive forever more.

For this perishable body must put on the imperishable, and this mortal body must put on immortality. When the perishable puts on the imperishable, and the mortal puts on immortality, then shall come to pass the saying that is written:

"Death is swallowed up in victory."
(1 Corinthians 15:53-54)

What a hope! And this hope literally changes us as we are focusing on that hope. If this promise of the resurrection is the source of our hope, we are being changed, results are happening. As you really believe that the Lord is going to come and he's going to resurrect you and you are going to be changed, that knowledge of the promise brings powerful results in your life. We are not just waiting for this to happen, but knowing it's going to happen, and looking forward to it happening, *that* is what begins to change you.

What kind of change does it make? Well, it makes you able to face everything differently. When you know that your hope is the reality of the resurrection, the manner in which you face everything in your life is altered. You face death differently. You have praise facing death.

When the perishable puts on the imperishable, and the mortal puts on immortality, then shall come to pass the saying that is written:

"Death is swallowed up in victory."
"O death, where is your victory?
    O death, where is your sting?"

The sting of death is sin, and the power of sin is the law. But thanks be to God, who gives us the victory through our Lord Jesus Christ.
(1 Corinthians 15:54-57)

Sin has been dealt with by Jesus. The power of sin is the law—the law we couldn't keep, the law we couldn't fulfill, the law we had broken. But Jesus took care of that too. He kept the law for us and he accepted death for us. And now we can face death saying, "Death, where is your victory? Death, where is your sting?"

I remember riding home from church one day, as a little boy. We had the windows down and a bee flew into our car. That bee landed on me and not thinking it through, I swatted at it, and all it did was make that bee mad. Very mad. He stung me on my hand and I shouted, "Ouch. That bee stung me!" and I started wailing and the bee flew around in the car.

Frantically, everyone in the car started waving and swatting at it. My family members had their Bibles out and they were flopping at the bee. Our car looked like a "Pentecostal Plymouth" heading down the road! There were Bibles and hands up in the air. You would not have thought we had been to a Baptist church service! Everyone in the car was terrified, but we were terrified of something that no longer posed any danger because the stinger was in my hand. And once a bee stings, it can't sting again.

Death flies around us. Death can scare us but let's think about this. Why should we fear death when the stinger of death has already been put into the hand of the Lord Jesus Christ? He has already overcome death.

Because of what Jesus did for us on the cross, we have *praise* facing death and we can have a *purpose* facing life. If you believe in the resurrection. If you believe that you are going to be changed. If you believe that you really are going to be different than you are now, it makes you desire to live differently and practice the process of transformation right now.

> Therefore, my beloved brothers, [because of the
> resurrection, because you will be changed,
> because your natural body is going to have a
> spiritual body, because Jesus is coming back
> and you're going to be changed in an atom of
> time in the twinkling of an eye, because death

has been conquered and it has no sting for you]
be steadfast, immovable, always abounding
in the work of the Lord, knowing that in the
Lord your labor is not in vain.
(1 Corinthians 15:58)

The idea that followers of Jesus should be content to simply wander through life until they get to the Promise Land, is absolutely not true. A person who has that attitude and that plan has never experienced the saving grace of Christ. They've never known the redeeming power of a new nature. A person who has been born again and has the hope of Christ, and eternal life, and the confidence of the resurrection and heaven says, "I want to live like I'm heading there right now."

Is that you? In your heart is there motivation to live a life as an image bearer of Christ? If we really believe he's coming, we should live with praise facing death, yes, and a purpose facing life, but also a purity facing Christ. We want to live a pure life because we know that Jesus is coming and we are going to see him. John, the last of the Apostles, wrote some incredibly beautiful and powerful words in 1 John 3:1-3:

See what kind of love the Father has given to us,
that we should be called children of God; and so
we are. The reason why the world does not

know us is that it did not know him. Beloved, we are God's children now, and what we will be has not yet appeared; but we know that when he appears we shall be like him, because we shall see him as he is. And everyone who thus hopes in him purifies himself as he is pure.

Wow! Think about that! What a revelation! Behold what manner of love the Father has given to us, that we should be called the children of God and that is who we are. That is who we *really* are. What an anticipation it is for us to think about what we will be when Jesus comes! We don't know exactly what we're going to be, but we do know that when he comes we will be like him. And we will see him as he is. What a motivation! It makes us want to live as children of God now. We purify ourselves not because we're afraid Jesus is going to condemn us. We are not trying to make ourselves acceptable to him. We are accepted in him by his grace and because we have this hope, we joyfully purify ourselves now.

Sometime ago, my wife Susan had surgery for a partial knee replacement, and she recovered very well. I was the "ice man" for a few weeks and I became one of the local convenient store's most faithful customers. During the recovery process, some ladies decided they would bring meals. They even set up a web page on the internet so you could see what was coming to the Polson's house for dinner. And guess what? My grown children found out about that web page. It was remarkable to see them suddenly show up on the doorstep because they had seen what was for supper that night. It was quite humbling for my wife and me to have the meals provided, and a little irritating to have our children eat them! But I noticed something. While we were waiting for the person to bring by the meal, we would look around to see if the house was tidy.

My wife is a wonderful housekeeper, and I'm sure your house *never* has any dishes in the sink or anything on the counter top. But a few minutes before our guests arrived with the food, I suddenly got interested in the plates and dishes lying about. I thought I would quickly clean up a bit. My wife Susan loved it. She sat on the sofa with ice on her knee, incapable of doing anything, just getting a kick out of watching me become suddenly interested in cleaning things up because company was coming over.

Well, I've got some news, friends. Company is coming. The King is coming. Maybe we need to tidy up a bit. The apostle John goes on to say that everyone who has this hope in Jesus purifies himself. It is the hope of seeing Jesus Christ and being with him that provides the motivation. It's all about him. Robinson's lyrics once again come to mind. "Come, thou Fount, come thou King: come thou precious Prince of Peace. Hear your bride, to you we sing, come, thou Fount of our blessing."

What a plan the Heavenly Father has provided for lives like ours, so marred by our selfishness and sin! By his amazing grace and the infinite love of Jesus, we have the privilege of restoration to the life we were intended to live. The life of a child of God, a life lived forever *In His Image*.

To him be the glory, forever and ever. Amen.

R.E.A.P. GUIDE

READ:

> 1 John 3:2-3
> Romans 8:18-25
> 1 Corinthians 15:50-58

EXAMINE:

1. What truth stood out to you from *In His Image*, Chapter 7? What do you most look forward to about heaven?
2. According to 1 John 3:2-3, when will we experience glorification? How should that hope motivate us now?
3. What will happen when we are glorified (Romans 8:21, 23)? How should that hope change how we live today (Romans 8:18)?
4. What will be the results when we are fully glorified (1 Corinthians 51, 54)? How should that hope motivate us now (1 Corinthians 15:58)?

APPLY:

- How have these passages challenged or encouraged you?
- For believers, one day the image of Christ will be fully ours. We will face no more pain, suffering or sin but will experience the full life with God we were originally created to experience. Is the future hope of your glorification meaningful to you?
- If that hope is not very meaningful to you right now, what would need to take place in your life to give you a longing for Christ and a longing for his image to be restored in you?

PRAY:

- Praise God for his commitment to you all your life long, to save you, sanctify you and ultimately glorify you.
- Ask Christ for a greater love for him and for his word, particularly for his promises to transform you.

AFTERWORD

As we have studied in this book, *In His Image*, we are to cooperate with God as he conforms us into the image of Christ. We are to devote ourselves to that process and to him. But we also have a responsibility to work with God in ways that can only be done all together. God calls you and me into worship along with other followers. Worship is to God alone, but it is while in the company of others where we make significant progress.

> Therefore, brothers, since we have confidence to
> enter the holy places by the blood of
> Jesus, by the new and living way that he opened
> for us through the curtain, that is, through his
> flesh, and since we have a great priest over the
> house of God, let us draw near with a true heart
> in full assurance of faith, with our

hearts sprinkled clean from an evil conscience and our bodies washed with pure water. Let us hold fast the confession of our hope without wavering, for he who promised is faithful. And let us consider how to stir up one another to love and good works, not neglecting to meet together, as is the habit of some, but encouraging one another, and all the more as you see the Day drawing near.
(Hebrews 10:19-25)

The writer of the book of Hebrews makes one point over and over—Jesus Christ is superior to everything that the Old Covenant had to offer. Christ and his work, makes all the works of the Old Covenant no longer necessary. He is the only sufficient way to approach God. So, as we focus on pursuing the image of Christ *together*, we know we are able to do this with an unshakeable confidence. God says that his people, whom he calls to himself together in public worship, can do so with confidence. We do not have to be doubtful in our attempts to follow after God because Jesus has opened the way to God, and he remains our high priest before God.

The book of Hebrews addresses the dependence that the Jewish people had on observing the sacrificial proportions of the law in order to be right with God and to fulfill and obey his commands. As we've studied, this careful observance of the law began back in the garden, when God created Adam and Eve and they sinned. God banished them from the garden and placed the cherubim with a flaming sword by the gate to keep God's people from coming back lest they die. Their only hope was for God to provide some means by which they could once again approach him.

God raised up one man, Abraham, and called him into a relationship with himself, and promised him, "I will multiply your offspring as the stars of heaven and will give to your offspring all these lands. And in your offspring, all the nations of the earth shall be blessed..." (Genesis 26:4). 400 years later there was a famine. All those descendants of Abraham traveled to Egypt, in order to get some help, and remained there, thanks to their connection to one man, Joseph.

But as time passed and hundreds of years went by, the king of Egypt no longer regarded Israel or its God, and had them trapped into slavery. God raised up another man, Moses, and called him to go into Egypt and challenge the king to "Let my people go" (Exodus 5, 8, 9, 10). Through many plagues, God delivered his people and called them out to Mount Sinai, where the law was given to them. In that law, God stipulated that they were to build a tabernacle to take with them on their exodus out of Egypt. In that tabernacle, they were to create a most holy place where God commanded them to build a seat for him—a throne on which he could sit, and he promised that he would journey with them and be with them. No one could go into the holy place, the presence of God, but a mediator who had carefully prepared himself according to God's law.

When Israel was established in the land of nations, a permanent temple was built which also contained a holy place. Inside, a curtain was hung to divide the people from the presence of God. On that curtain, which was 60 feet high, 30 feet wide, and four feet thick were images of the cherubim. Those images reminded us that the way back to the garden had been cut off. Access to God was forbidden. Only one purified man, one time of year, carrying the sacrificial blood to sprinkle on the altar, could enter.

When Jesus came, there was another temple that Herod had reconstructed because the first had been destroyed. It too had a curtain that divided the people from unrestrained access to God. When Christ Jesus died on the cross, that 60' high, 30' wide, 4' thick temple curtain was ripped from the top to the bottom (Matthew 27:51). When Jesus breathed out his last breath and said, "It is finished" (John 19:30), all of the work that was required for man to have access to God, was complete. Finished. Done. Jesus did it, and he did it by shedding his blood. This is the confidence that we have. The writer of the letter of Hebrews was encouraging God's people to press in and to reject anything that did not bring them to Christ. They could now pursue Jesus with a true heart, full of devotion and faith.

But the confidence for God's people today is even greater. As the church body, our confidence is not just that the way is open and we can get in. Our confidence is in the fact that Jesus still reigns alive today and he remains our high priest. Hebrews 7:25 reads, "Consequently, he is able to save to the uttermost those who draw near to God through him, since he always lives to make intercession for them."

All the points in Hebrews leading up to this section of Scripture state that Jesus is fully acquainted with every one of our weaknesses. He experienced temptation just like you and me. The fact that Jesus never sinned doesn't make him an unsympathetic savior; it makes him the only Savior. Had he sinned, he would have been just like us. Since he did not sin, he is able to understand, with mercy, our plight. This makes Jesus a sympathetic priest on our behalf so we can have confidence that we will always have access to God.

There is nothing you can do to keep yourself in the grace of God. Jesus did it all, and will continue to minister to you forever. If you have come to God through Jesus, you belong to God. He has sought you out and he will never abandon you. This is the source of our confidence.

Hebrews 10, verse 22 contains the first of the phrases, "Let us draw near with a true heart…" Verse 23, again, "Let us hold fast…" Verse 24, "Let us consider how to stir up one another…" The language is not singular; it's "Let *us*." We have a role to play *together*.

The first of the two, "Let us…" applications is this: "Let us draw near to God in faith with a true heart full of devotion to God." God calls us into corporate worship, and asks us to come with a heart that is genuine, and not for our own purposes. God alone is to be our focus.

The second "Let us…" is this: "Let us hold fast the confession of our hope without wavering, for he who promised is faithful (Hebrews 10:23). In the book of Hebrews up to this point, there has been a thread of hope that has united these texts. Jesus is superior in every way. He is the sacrifice for our sins. He is the living priest who ministers to us and for us, in the presence of God.

When the Bible speaks of hope in Hebrews 6, it talks about hope as an *anchor*.

> We have this as a sure and steadfast *anchor* of
> the soul, a hope that enters into the inner place
> behind the curtain, where Jesus has gone as a
> forerunner on our behalf, having become a high
> priest forever after the order of Melchizedek.
> (Hebrews 6:19-20)

So often we speak of hope as this uncertain future that we're "kind of" thinking might come to pass. As inconsequential as our lives seem right now, we're just looking for that next big break, that next big opportunity. If this year's been tough, we hope that next year will be a little better.

I read recently that a professor at New York University polled 3,000 people asking them, "What do have you to live for?" He was shocked to discover that 94 percent were simply enduring the present while they waited for a better future. We Christians live for the reality of what has already been done. Jesus as our forerunner has gone into the holy place of God, where he reigns, and Jesus is there now. He is holding on to us. When I fear that my hope is no better than those polled by this New York University professor, I am reminded by my fellow believers that my hope is in Christ who holds me fast.

If you do not have love for Jesus Christ and know that he is holding you fast, say to him now, "I believe in what you've accomplished for me on the cross. I am a sinner and need you to save me and be my King. Forgive me, and thank you for what you have done." This is the beginning of a relationship based on fact and truth of who Jesus is and what he has done for us.

The third "Let us," is found in Hebrews 10:24-25:

> And let us consider how to *stir up* one another
> to love and good works, not neglecting to meet
> together, as is the habit of some, but
> encouraging one another, and all the more as
> you see the Day drawing near.

"To stir up" comes from a Greek word which in the English is *paroxysm*. Paroxysm means "a violent fit," an eruption of shaking. It's like taking a Taser to your brother or sister in the church and zapping them. In other words, we are to figure out how we can be a sudden eruption of love and good works in a way that is helpful to our fellow Christians.

The confidence we *feel* we need in order to encourage our fellow Christians or witness to unbelievers does not need to come from ourselves, but instead from the one who made us *In His Image.* God sent his Son to accomplish for us what we could never have done for ourselves. And now, as we are being restored in his image, we find ourselves fully equipped for every good work (2 Timothy 3:17).

Joe Kappel
Pastor of Adult Ministries
West Park Baptist Church
Knoxville, Tennessee

What people are saying about
In His Image...

"In the writing of *In His Image,* Pastor Polson not only does a wonderful job showing us what it means to be made in the image of God, but he also provides us with very practical steps that will help us in this transformation process. I think you will find this book to be a positive step in seeing God transform you into His image!"
— *Mark Kirk, Pastor of Calvary Knoxville*
(Knoxville, Tennessee)

"In a culture awash with self-identity talk, Pastor Sam Polson directs us to the truest identity of all—our Creator and Redeemer, the Lord Jesus Christ Himself. By successfully combining insightful theology and pastoral warmth, *In His Image* will enrich the reader's walk with God. I can see this book being particularly helpful for any Sunday school class, small group meeting, or in-home Bible study."
— *Dr. Greg Baker, Pastor of Fellowship Bible Church*
(Liberty, Utah)

"Beyond the profound and fascinating way in which Pastor Sam Polson takes us along the thread of the significance and practical implications of the theme of God's image in Scripture, *In His Image* is a book that springs as much from the study and living out of those truths, as from a rich experience of pastoral service. The book awakens us to a simple truth, old but always relevant, that the purpose and passion of God is seeing humans transformed in His image, an image fully revealed in Christ. This is the fundamental challenge of the Gospel, to which no one can remain neutral. Pastor Sam endeared Romania (together with his wife Susan they have a son adopted from Suceava), has been involved for many years together with West Park Baptist Church in Christian mission in our country, and I am honored by his friendship and service together. I am grateful that *In His Image* is available in Romanian."

— *Pastor Eugen Groza, Bethany Baptist Church*
(Timişoara, Romania)

"Each of us lives our daily lives based on how we answer two essential human questions, 'Who am I?' and 'Why am I here?' *In His Image* invites us to revisit and reframe our answers to these foundational questions. For readers who have ears to hear the Spirit speak through His Word, there is the promise of new life in the present and new hope for the future as we gain new perspectives on what it means to be fully human in Christ."

— *Rick Dunn, Pastor of Fellowship Church Knoxville*
(Knoxville, Tennessee)

"Coram Deo is a Latin phrase translated in the presence of God, and defines how my friend Sam Polson submits to Christ and His kingdom. In this book, Pastor Sam provides a fresh and stimulating insight into the beautiful, biblical doctrine of Imago Dei, the image of God, while giving the reader the tools needed to REAP the word. *In His Image* is a book I highly recommend to assist in family worship, private devotion, or personal study."

— *Dr. David Trempe, Pastor of Westminster Chapel*
(Knoxville, Tennessee)

"In the book *In His Image*, Sam Polson carries the reader on a journey that challenges us to realize our destiny and purpose for life. As 'iron sharpeneth iron' we find ways to appreciate and respect God's image in others through the mirror of the Word. Pastor Polson also challenges us to realize how the enemy desires to mar Christ's image in our quest to reveal Him to the world. I challenge you to read and grow into the likeness of our Creator and Redeemer. *In His Image* will inspire, educate, and guide you in that sacred process."

— *Rev. Sam Phillips, Church of God*
(Cleveland, Tennessee)

ABOUT CLIMBING ANGEL PUBLISHING

Climbing Angel Publishing exists for the purpose of sharing stories of hope and encouragement, aiding in the gathering together of community, and supporting the process of betterment. The following books are available at www.ClimbingAngel.com, Amazon.com, and major bookstores.

Adult Books: *(Romans 8:28-30)*

In His Image

Children's Books: *(Philippians 4:8)*

The Christmas Tree Angel
The Unmade Moose
Thump
Somebunny To Love

CPSIA information can be obtained
at www.ICGtesting.com
Printed in the USA
LVHW01s0449280917
550339LV00001B/1/P